GEOGRAPHY BEE DEMYSTIFIED

GEOGRAPHY BEE DEMYSTIFIED

A Preparation Guide
for the
State and National Geography Bees

THIRD EDITION (REVISED)

Ram Iyer

Edited by
SMITHA GUNDAVAJHALA

CONTENTS

PREFACE TO THE THIRD EDITION

The second edition of *Geography Bee Demystified* appeared in February 2009, and it met with greater success than the first. In the third edition, thanks to suggestions and input from participants of the 2008, 2009 and 2010 geography bees, I have been able to improve upon previous versions by updating some information and adding extra questions that will keep up with changes in 2010-2011.

Some participants requested that I include a section on **Cultural Geography,** which I have done. In the past, many have also asked me to include more state-level and school-level questions. In response, I introduced a new guide in 2010, *Geography Bee Simplified,* that would cater to the School Bee and some rounds of the State Bee. The *Geography Bee Demystified* series continues to focus on the State Bee and the Nationals, although some of the questions in this book could still be applicable to the School Bee. In addition, I've revised the Current Affairs section, disposing of outdated questions. The geographic components of each Current Affairs question from the last edition have been incorporated into their respective categories so that the information is not lost. Several new questions have been added to all sections, from that of the United States to Physical Geography.

Some helpful hints

This is an unofficial guide to the National Geographic Bee and the rules and format of the Bee are subject to change. While questions in

Current Affairs and Physical Geography have played a major role in past bees, there is no guarantee this will be the trend forever. US Geography has started to play a significant role in the School and the State Bees. Generally, US geography is not a category at the national level. However, questions that are not biased toward particular states could still find their way into the Nationals. The National Geographic Society could always throw in a surprise or two. All participants who use this guide should be aware of that. I have not included any maps because there is no match for the maps provided by the National Geographic Society. In fact, there is no way around that requirement if you intend to be successful. Students who have found this guide most useful are those who study this guide with a National Geographic Atlas in front of them. Whatever the format of the bee, the knowledge gained from using this book will help a participant perform better in this year's bee than they have in the last one.

As in the first edition and second editions, I have made every effort towards making sure the questions do not resemble any I encountered when my boys were involved in the bees in 2006 and 2007. Efforts have also been made to make sure that none of the questions released by the National Geographic Society to the press since 2008 are included in this guide. If there are similarities, it has more to do with the use of similar sources than anything else. I have used National Geographic resources extensively. Students should also realize that the environment in 2010-2011 is very different from that of earlier years and the past is not a guide to the type of questions that could be asked in 2010-2011. The world is changing as you read this.

Several reviewers advised me to include maps to transform this guide into a complete book. While some maps may be included in later versions, a geography bee participant has access to top-quality atlases from the National Geographic Society and other sources, and a map or two in this guide would not help much. This is a guide written for a serious geography participant who is already aware of the basic facts. The reader is advised to use this guide in tandem with popular atlases to get the best result. A serious contestant, as always, should study all available resources in the market, including this one! There is no magic solution for doing well in the geography bee. You need your favorite reference materials handy as you read this guide.

Why choose to use this guide?

There is no shortage of geography bee preparation materials in the market. While most available materials lay the basic foundation, *Geography Bee Demystified* takes bee preparation to a higher level. It focuses on the thought processes necessary to tie together the vast geographic knowledge needed to answer tough questions.

Who is this guide for?

This guide is for serious contestants. It is for those who already have mastered the basic facts, who have a good shot at the state-level and national-level competitions. Participants in the final round of the school bee and winners who will take the state qualification tests will also benefit immensely from using this book.

How is the guide organized?

Geography Bee Demystified is divided into ten chapters based primarily on the continents of the world. There are some adjustments, as in the case of a transcontinental country like Russia, which is included under the chapter "Asia." The question-and-answer format lends itself to an easier way of preparation for those who have limited time to prepare for the geography bee.

How do I use this guide?

This guide is most useful with the companionship of a good atlas, such as those published by the National Geographic Society, Dorling Kindersley Publishing, and Kingfisher Publishing.

I have had the good fortune of watching the state and the national bees up close. Does this guide contain actual questions from those competitions?

The answer is "no." Although the guide is written to help prepare for the competitions, using the exact questions from the competitions not only is unethical but would also defeat the very purpose behind the National Geographic Society's competitions. The goal of the National Geographic Society is to increase geography awareness around the country. The competition does not lend itself to a "cramming" session. Instead, it seeks to develop an appreciation of geography. If you have had some experience listening to many of the questions asked, you will realize that the wealth of knowledge delivered through the medium of these questions is probably more educational than the question itself. For example, you will rarely find a question that merely asks," What is the capital of Germany?" Instead, what you will hear is a wealth of information about Berlin delivered along with the obvious question in the competition. In keeping with that spirit, I have done my best to avoid questions that resemble what I have already seen or heard. If there are similarities to some of the questions from past competitions, it is purely a coincidence. Some of the questions are from the notes my son compiled from books and television shows while preparing for the geography bee. It is highly likely that some of the information he gathered appeared in the competitions in some form. I have also made an effort to frame the questions in a way that continues to develop the thought process necessary to do well in these nerve-racking competitions.

Do these competitions have an element of luck involved?

To be truthful, yes. The best way to combat the "luck" factor is through preparation over a long period of time using multiple resources. Despite all best efforts, many brilliant students do catch a bad break. I believe that, with some luck, any participant who has made it to the top ten in the state and national championships, and participants who barely missed making that cut, could have been a winner under different circumstances. What this means is the fact that at least 15 to 20 participants are evenly matched in these competitions. Whatever the result of the competition may be, the experience gained is invaluable and worth a try! Don't let the disappointments stop you! Ultimately, the knowledge gained and the actual application of that knowledge, later in life, will result in all the participants winning again and again in real life.

How do I prepare? I have other classes, I have a busy schedule at school, and my parents work late.

This is a fact of life. In fact, for most students, the end of the school year coincides with the Nationals competition. The earlier you prepare the better. This guide has been written with a view to give participants, under these conditions, some help in developing a game plan. The busy schedule of the parents plays a part in how much help a participant gets. Some schools do provide extra help in these circumstances. Despite best efforts, the playing field cannot be leveled for all situations and circumstances. One can start by referring to all the books that are available in the market several months before the competitions start. The local library is a great resource. In addition, use this guide to supplement your knowledge. To get the best out of this guide, you have to surround yourself with all the atlases and books you have, physically locate the answer to each questions on the map, and then try to read more about it in your resources. As you locate a place, try to see what is around that location. Often times, questions in these competitions tend to use the surrounding places or physical terrain in the adjacent areas as hints. Very seldom will you find a question stated exactly as what you find in the books you have. In other words, you have to know your geography, not just the answers.

How do I prepare for the Physical Geography questions?

This category is always a stressful one for competitors. In the state bees, this category is manageable with some moderate-level preparation and the questions are not that hard. In the qualifying rounds for the national bee, however, physical geography questions could often eliminate very knowledgeable participants. Again, preparation is the best way to balance out the luck factor. To succeed, mastery over your earth science textbook, at the very least, is a must. Borrow the book from your school and read ahead of your class. In addition, if you make it to the Nationals, *The National Geographic Desk Reference* is a great resource. Granted, this may not be sufficient. Any term in hydrology and glaciology could be asked. Be aware of what is happening in the world. Terms that deal with weather, climatology, and meteorology are likely to gain more prominence as issues related to climate change bubble up in importance. Luckily, there are several books on all these categories available at your junior-high library or at your local public library.

How do I prepare for the Current Affairs category?

In this category, questions are formulated with several geographic location hints. At first glance, it might seem like a game of luck. In reality, questions are framed in a very fair manner and hints are abundant. Keeping up with current affairs, however, does help. It will not only boost your confidence but will also reduce the luck factor significantly. Be aware that fourth graders might be competing with eighth graders, and the personnel in charge of making questions will not be unfair to the fourth graders. Keeping up with current affairs also helps in the "non–current affair" categories. Occasionally, despite best efforts, you may run into "where did they get that?" types of questions. However, 99% of the time, questions are based on events that happened over the past two years. In the state bee, this category could make or break your chances of getting into the final ten. At the very least, you need to be aware of important news items from the past four months.

What did the pronouncer say?

Let's face it— it is virtually impossible for a pronouncer to pronounce a name in another language as clearly as a native would. What should you do if you are not sure what you heard? Use your quota of "repeats." Do not, however, waste your repository of repeats by asking the pronouncer merely to repeat the question. Often, you did hear the question right the first time! Instead, ask the pronouncer to spell it. You may be shocked to find that you had known the answer all along.

Use your allotted time.

You have 12 seconds to answer a question. Use it. Do not start answering a question until you are in the seventh second. The same applies to the state bee qualifying test. If you finish the written test early, read your answers again. In populous states like California and New York, this could be critical. There are no bonus points for finishing early.

The information provided in this guide is based on my own research and that of other participants who studied for the geography bee. It is not guaranteed to be without inaccuracies. If you find any errors as you use this guide, please bring them to my attention so that future editions and subsequent versions can be improved. Please state your sources when you send a correction.

Please visit **http://www.geographybee-coaching.com/** to send your suggestions or corrections. This site may also have **new announcements, updates, corrections, and new quizzes.**

ACKNOWLEDGMENTS

I would like to thank all past and current Geography Bee participants and their parents for having played a major role in motivating me to continue to work on revisions to past editions of this guide. Without their encouragement, I would not be able to expand upon my previous editions. I also want to thank my family, friends, the local Kansas City–area community, and well-wishers from the North South Foundation, an all-volunteer organization that encourages excellence in education, for having played a major part when I was writing the first edition of this study guide. I want to thank my two boys, Suneil and Eswar, who are busy with their own academic lives, but continue to help when required. The Johnson County Public Libraries, Kansas, also need a special mention for carrying and honoring our transfer requests for all the books necessary for research in preparation for a competition of this nature. The quality of participants in the 2010-2011 geography bees continues to amaze me. A special thank you goes out to these participants. I would also like to thank Smitha Gundavajhala, editor of *Geography Bee Simplified*, who helped me edit this guide and provided valuable input and suggestions when needed. I also want to thank the parents of a Geography Bee participant who helped edit the second edition of this guide and who continues to provide valuable input when needed.

My two boys, Eswar and Suneil, continue to make valuable suggestions. We have, however, expanded our circle of friends and have a new generation of geography enthusiasts, outside of my immediate family members, who are making the process even more exciting than ever before. Their input is greatly appreciated. I want to thank them for their help in improving upon the second edition.

CHAPTER 1

The United States

1. Name the 1,267-foot peak near the Belle Fourche River that in
    1906 was proclaimed the first national monument by President
    Roosevelt.
    Devils Tower

2. During the Revolutionary War, Americans led by Benedict
    Arnold and Ethan Allen captured the fort of Ticonderoga in what
    US state?
    New York

3. On June 17, 1775, Americans and British clashed in a famous
    battle just outside Boston, Massachusetts. Name this battle.
    Battle of Bunker Hill

4. Name the river that cuts through the Rocky Mountains at Hells
    Canyon on the Idaho-Oregon border.
    Snake River

5. The 4,700-year-old Mendocino Tree is found at Montgomery
    Woods State Reserve in what coastal US state?
    California

6. Adjuntas is a mountainous region on an island that is a major
    producer of coffee. Name this island in the Caribbean that has
    Ponce as one of its major cities.
    Puerto Rico

7. What river forms part of the boundary between New York and
    Pennsylvania?
    Delaware River

8. Mount Marcy, at 5,344 feet, is the highest point in the state of
    New York. This peak is in what mountain range in northeastern
    New York?
    Adirondack Mountains

9. What US state that borders Quebec has the shortest coastline on any ocean?
New Hampshire

10. Basketball was invented in what US state that borders Rhode Island?
Massachusetts

11. The Elizabeth Islands in Massachusetts lie between Buzzards Bay and what body of water to its south?
Vineyard Sound

12. The Mason-Dixon Line was named after the surveyors who drew the boundary between what two US states?
Maryland and Pennsylvania

13. California's Bay Bridge connects what two cities?
Oakland and San Francisco

14. Name Indiana's second-largest city, located at the confluence of the St. Joseph, St. Marys, and the Maumee Rivers.
Fort Wayne

15. The Wyandotte Caves, one of the largest caverns in the country, are located in what state bordering Kentucky and Michigan?
Indiana

16. In 1861, bombardment of what fort on Charleston Harbor marked the opening engagement of the American Civil War?
Fort Sumter

17. New Harmony, site of the early headquarters of the US Geological Survey, is situated near what river in Indiana?
Wabash River

18. Name the channel that lies east of West Quoddy Head, the easternmost point in the lower 48 States, separating mainland Maine from an island of the same name as that of the channel in southern New Brunswick, Canada.
Grand Manan Channel

19. During the Pony Penning Carnival, in the month of July, several wild ponies are made to swim 200 yards south from Assateague, Maryland, to the island of Chincoteague in what US state?
Virginia

20. The National Hurricane Center is located in what city bordered by the Biscayne National Park to the east?
Miami

21. What river that has its source near the Okefenokee Swamp forms part of the border between Florida and Georgia?
St. Marys River

22. An aquifer exists under the Great Plains states from Texas all the way up to South Dakota. Name this aquifer.
Ogallala Aquifer

23. The Missouri River meets its largest tributary just east of the Montana–North Dakota border. Name this tributary.
Yellowstone River

24. The Absaroka Range, in northwest Wyoming, crosses into what other state?
Montana

25. In 1952, rich deposits of uranium near Moab brought major investment to what state?
Utah

26. Ernest Hemingway Memorial, northeast of Ketchum, is in what US state?
Idaho

27. Stellwagen Bank National Marine Sanctuary sits at the mouth of what US bay in the northeast?
Massachusetts Bay

28. Land Between the Lakes National Recreation Area lies between Lake Barkley and what lake in the southeastern United States?
Kentucky Lake

29. What river marks Florida's western border with Alabama?
Perdido River

30. Sumter National Forest is in what US state east of Georgia?
South Carolina

31. Raleigh, Durham, and what other city form North Carolina's Research Triangle?
Chapel Hill

32. Battle Creek, Michigan, is situated at the confluence of Battle Creek and what other major river?
Kalamazoo River

33. What river links Lake Erie to Lake St. Clair?
Detroit River

34. Name the lake that lies at the point where Tennessee, Mississippi, and Alabama meet.
Pickwick Lake

35. Rhythm-and-blues singer Ray Charles was born in Albany, a city on the banks of the Flint River in what state that has Cumberland Island as its southernmost barrier island?
Georgia

36. Famous writer Helen Keller was born near Florence, a city on the Tennessee River. Florence is located in the northwest corner of what state that borders Florida and Mississippi?
Alabama

37. George C. Marshall Space Flight Center, NASA's first headquarters, was built in northern Alabama's largest city. Name this city.
Huntsville

38. Cherokee National Forest lies in the foothills of what US mountain system?
Appalachian Mountains

39. Breton National Wildlife Reserve is in what US state?
Louisiana

40. What US state has the Great Egg Harbor River?
New Jersey

41. What river forms the boundary between Georgia and South Carolina?
Savannah River

42. Rat Island is part of what major island chain in Alaska?
Aleutian Islands

43. What US state, which has the city of Macon, is home to well-known Stone Mountain Park?
Georgia

44. Dahlonega, the site of the first US gold rush in 1828 and 1829, lies south of the Blue Ridge Mountains in what US state?
Georgia

45. Okefenokee is a wetland region shared by Georgia and what state?
Florida

46. Name the smallest mainland US state west of the Mississippi River whose natural hot springs in the Ouachita Mountains are a major tourist attraction.
Arkansas

47. Name the plateau south of the Missouri River in the state of Missouri that extends southwest into northern Arkansas, north of the Arkansas River and west of the Black River, and also into northeast Oklahoma.
Ozark Plateau

48. Superior National Forest in Minnesota lies to the northeast of what mountain range?
Mesabi Range

49. An imperfect survey in the 1783 Treaty of Paris resulted in an area of land on the Canadian side of Lake of the Woods in Minnesota being made part of the United States. Name this region.
Northwest Angle

50. What town, south of Springfield, Missouri, is considered a music city as Nashville, Tennessee, is?
Branson

51. The Pascagoula River is in what US state?
Mississippi

52. Name Tennessee's largest city on the Mississippi River.
Memphis

53. Name the famous Texas city that was founded as a Spanish mission in 1718.
San Antonio

54. The Sabine River forms most of the border between Texas and what state?
Louisiana

55. What present-day US state, bordered by the Connecticut River to its east, was an independent country from 1777 to 1791?
Vermont

56. The British colonized a region in what present-day US state by building a settlement on the St. Mary's River?
Maryland

57. The largest freshwater port in the world is in what city on the Delaware River?
Philadelphia

58. Mohawks, Oneidas, Onondagas, Cayugas, and Senecas were the original inhabitants of what US state?
New York

59. The Delaware River forms the western border and the Hudson River forms the northeastern border of a state on the Atlantic coast. Name this US state.
New Jersey

60. Mennonites from Russia brought Turkey Red Wheat to a region in the United States, where it later became the main crop. Name this region.
Great Plains

61. Chimney Rock, a sandstone pinnacle in the state of Nebraska, is near what tributary of the Missouri River?
Platte River

62. In 1872, on the first Arbor Day, over a million trees were planted in a state whose present-day forests owe their existence to this day. Name this state that borders Wyoming and Missouri.
Nebraska

63. In 1770, Ethan Allen formed the revolutionary Green Mountain Boys to fight the New Yorkers in what state?
Vermont

64. Carlsbad Caverns National Park in New Mexico lies within what mountains?
Guadalupe Mountains

65. One can find an ancient site of pueblo ruins and cliff dwellings in Cibola County in what US state that borders Oklahoma and Arizona?
New Mexico

66. Organ Pipe Cactus National Monument is in what state that borders Mexico and Nevada?
Arizona

67. In 1945, the world's first nuclear weapon was detonated at White Sands in what US state?
New Mexico

68. In 1836, during the war for independence from Mexico, a San Antonio mission that had been transformed into a makeshift fort was besieged by Mexican troops and every American in it was killed. Name this fort.
Alamo

69. Davy Crockett's birthplace is in what state whose capital lies on the Cumberland River?
Tennessee

70. Frenchman Flat and Yucca Flat, sites used for testing nuclear weapons in 1951, are in what western US state?
Nevada

71. The lowest place in the Western Hemisphere, Death Valley, straddles the border between California and what other US state?
Nevada

72. Toledo, Ohio, lies near the mouth of what river on Lake Erie?
Maumee River

73. In Wyoming, sixty million years ago, molten lava forced its way up through sandstone rock. After cooling and erosion, what now remains is a 1,267-foot column of rock. Name this tourist site.
Devils Tower

74. The best-preserved cliff dwellings in the United States are found at Mesa Verde National Park in what state?
Colorado

75. Rainbow Bridge, one of the world's largest natural bridges, is found in a US state that borders Wyoming and Colorado. Name this state.
Utah

76. The Civil Rights Movement is often associated with the town of Selma. This town lies on what river?
Alabama River

77. Lake Winnebago, a large freshwater lake where iceboat races are held in winter, is in what US state on Lake Superior?
Wisconsin

78. Which state does not border Lake Michigan: Illinois, Minnesota, or Wisconsin?
Minnesota

79. What river flows through the Canadian towns of Dawson and Whitehorse and the US town of Tanana?
Yukon River

80. What is the world's longest southward-flowing river system?
Mississippi-Missouri River

81. At 12,799 feet, what is Montana's highest point?
Granite Peak

82. The historic Custer's Last Stand, an armed engagement in 1876 between a Lakota–Northern Cheyenne combined force and the US Army, was fought near what river?
Little Big Horn

83. What city in Maine lies near the Kennebec River?
Augusta

84. Because of its natural resources, what state is known as the Bonanza State?
Montana

85. The St. Croix River forms part of the border between Minnesota and what state?
Wisconsin

86.   If you are near the southeastern region of the Santiago Mountains, on the US-Mexican border, you are in what state?
       Texas

87.   Which state lies farther east, Georgia or North Carolina?
       North Carolina

88.   The US state capital of Topeka lies on what river?
       Kansas River

89.   San Joaquin Valley and Mt. Shasta are in what US state?
       California

90.   At Mono Lake, spectacular tufa towers, or calcium carbonate spires, are formed by the interaction of freshwater springs with the salty lake water. These towers are found in what western US state?
       California

91.   Times Square is on what island on the US East Coast?
       Manhattan Island

92.   In 1778, Captain James Cook landed on an island and named it after John Montagu, the fourth Earl of Sandwich. Name this island.
       Kauai, Hawaii

93.   On January 24, 1848, James Marshall discovered gold at Sutter's Mill in Coloma in what US state?
       California

94.   "Black Thursday," October 29, 1929, when the US stock market crashed, marked the beginning of a major economic downturn. This downturn is often referred to as what period in the country's history?
       Great Depression

95. What is the only US state capital that is accessible only by air and water?
Juneau

96. What US capital city lies near the confluence of the Elk and Kanawha Rivers?
Charleston

97. The only major diamond field in the United States is in what state?
Arkansas

98. The highest auto road in the United States is in what state?
Colorado

99. Wilmington, often known as the chemical capital of the world, is in what state that first adopted the US Constitution, on December 7, 1787?
Delaware

100. The oldest city in the United States was settled in 1565. Name this city.
St. Augustine, Florida

101. In 1793, Eli Whitney invented the cotton gin in what state that is also known for the invention of Coca-Cola?
Georgia

102. In 1863, the Emancipation Proclamation was signed in a state that is nicknamed the Prairie State. Name this state.
Illinois

103. The city of Huntington, West Virginia, lies near what bordering state?
Ohio

104. Jeffboat, on the Ohio River, is the largest inland shipbuilder in the United States. This company is located in Jeffersonville in what state?
Indiana

105. What state produced the first tractor and is nicknamed the Hawkeye State?
Iowa

106. What US state discovered helium and is home to the first woman to fly across the Atlantic Ocean?
Kansas

107. What US gulf state, whose Acadian region is dominated by the Cajun culture, is one of the leading producers of salt?
Louisiana

108. What Maryland city housed the first US telegraph line?
Baltimore

109. Which US city on the Atlantic is often called the "Cradle of Liberty"?
Boston

110. Craters of the Moon National Monument is in what state that has Pend Oreille Lake in its panhandle region?
Idaho

111. The world's largest limestone quarry is in what US state?
Michigan

112. The historic Pony Express headed westward from St. Joseph in what US state?
Missouri

113. In 1853, what US state separated from Oregon Territory?
Washington

114. Rapid City is located just north of what famous US landmark?
Mount Rushmore

115. The driest US state is home to one of the largest manmade lakes in the world. Name this state.
Nevada

116. The city of Pueblo, Colorado, lies on what river?
Arkansas River

117. What was the first US state to declare its independence from England?
New Hampshire

118. The oldest and longest continuously used US highway, the El Camino Real, is a National Historic Trail that is one of the newest state monuments. Dedicated in November 2005, this is in what state?
New Mexico

119. Garrison Dam, the world's fifth-largest earthen dam, on the Missouri River, is in what US state that is nicknamed the "The Peace Garden State"?
North Dakota

120. The Capitol building of this US state, the leading iodine producer in the country, sits on a major oil field. Name this state.
Oklahoma

121. The Union Jack flew as the unofficial flag of what present-day US state that was annexed to the United States in 1898?
Hawaii

122.   Vandalia was the capital of what US state, bordering Lake
        Michigan and Kentucky, before the state established its new
        capital in 1837?
        Illinois

123.   The Alenuihaha Channel separates Maui from what island that
        was formed from five shield volcanoes?
        The Big Island (Hawaii Island)

124.   Shreveport, Louisiana, lies on what tributary of the Mississippi
        River?
        Red River

125.   What city in Arizona lies at the confluence of the Gila and the
        Colorado Rivers?
        Yuma

126.   The state capital of Little Rock is situated on what river?
        Arkansas

127.   The town of Gary, Indiana, lies near what lake?
        Lake Michigan

128.   The capital city of Utah lies near what lake?
        Great Salt Lake

129.   The Kodiak bear, world's largest sub-species of bear, is found in
        what US state?
        Alaska

130.   Geronimo, the legendary leader of the Apaches, was one of the last
        to surrender to US troops in Skeleton Canyon in what US state?
        Arizona

131. What mountain range runs along the western coast of California?
Coast Range

132. Name the saltwater lake that is situated in southern California.
Salton Sea

133. Dover, Delaware, lies on what river?
St. Jones River

134. Kotzebue Sound and Cook Inlet are bodies of water in what US state?
Alaska

135. What US state extends into the Eastern Hemisphere?
Alaska

136. In 1937, philanthropist Solomon R. Guggenheim and artist Hilla von Rebay started a foundation that built the famous Guggenheim Museum to help artists and writers. This museum is in what US city?
New York City

137. Attu Island is the westernmost and largest island of what island group in the Aleutian Islands of Alaska—Near Islands or Fox Islands?
Near Islands

138. Kenai Peninsula is closest to what major Alaskan city?
Anchorage

139. Name the Alaskan peninsula that juts out between Norton Sound and Kotzebue Sound.
Seward Peninsula

140.   Isle Royale, the largest island in Lake Superior, is part of what US state?
        Michigan

141.   The Red River forms part of the border between Oklahoma and what US state?
        Texas

142.   What river forms most of the border between South Carolina and Georgia?
        Savannah River

143.   What river forms the boundary between Vermont and New Hampshire?
        Connecticut River

144.   What river forms part of the boundary between Illinois and Indiana?
        Wabash River

145.   What US state has the Salmon River Mountains?
        Idaho

146.   What mountain range runs along the Montana-Idaho border?
        Bitterroot Range

147.   The city of Waco, Texas, lies on what river?
        Brazos River

148.   Name the largest desert in the United States, which lies mainly in Nevada and Utah.
        The Great Basin

149.   The Three Patriarchs, sandstone cliffs named Abraham, Isaac, and Jacob, can be found in what US national park near the Virgin River?
        Zion National Park

150. The township of Pelee, the southernmost point in Canada, lies very close to what city in Ohio?
Sandusky

151. The city of Austin, Texas, lies on what river?
Colorado River

152. Zion National Park, just southeast of the Escalante Desert, is in what US state?
Utah

153. In 1869, the world's first transcontinental railroad joined east to west in what Utah city just north of the Great Salt Lake?
Promontory

154. What Vermont city lies on the Winooski River?
Montpelier

155. Shenandoah Valley in Virginia is in what mountain range?
Blue Ridge Mountains

156. Richmond, Virginia, lies on what river?
James River

157. Grand Coulee Dam in Washington lies on the northern reaches of what plateau?
Columbia Plateau

158. The San Juan Islands lie to the northwest of what US state?
Washington

159. What Washington city has the world's tallest totem pole, standing at 105 feet high?
Tacoma

160. The Tug Fork River forms part of the boundary between Kentucky and what other US state that was admitted to the Union on June 20, 1863, as the 35th state?
West Virginia

161. The city of Harpers Ferry lies at the point where the states of West Virginia, Virginia, and Maryland meet. This West Virginian city lies at the confluence of the Potomac and what other river?
Shenandoah River

162. In 1902, one of the largest meteorites ever found in the United States was discovered in Willamette Valley in what state?
Oregon

163. What mountains run along part of the border between Oregon and California?
Klamath Mountains

164. The city of Philadelphia, Pennsylvania, lies on what river?
Delaware River

165. The Ohio River is formed by the confluence of the Monongahela and what other river at Pittsburgh, Pennsylvania?
Allegheny River

166. Lake Marion is the largest lake in what US state?
South Carolina

167. Kings Peak, at 13,528 feet, is the highest peak on what mountain range in northeastern Utah?
Uinta Mountains

168. The Lower Fox River connects the city of Green Bay, Wisconsin, with what body of water?
Lake Winnebago

169. Name the 3,860-square-mile closed drainage basin in south-central Wyoming where water flows neither east nor west.
Great Divide Basin

170. At 7,731 feet above sea level, this lake is the largest high-altitude lake in the United States. Name this lake.
Yellowstone Lake

171. The world's largest radio telescope lies near the mouth of what river in Puerto Rico?
Arecibo River

172. The Outer Banks, long sandbars that have resulted in many shipwrecks, lie off the coast of what US state?
North Carolina

173. The city of Fort Collins, Colorado, is closest to what major city in Wyoming?
Cheyenne

174. The cities of Winston-Salem and Greensboro lie on what plateau in North Carolina?
Piedmont Plateau

175. The US Air Force Academy is located just north of what major city in Colorado?
Colorado Springs

176. Cooperstown, home of the National Baseball Hall of Fame, is in what US state?
New York

177. Name the US town in the Adirondack Mountains that was the site of the 1932 and the 1980 Winter Olympics.
Lake Placid

178. A modern US state capital city, at 7,000 feet above sea level, has been inhabited since 1610, making this city the highest state capital and the longest inhabited state capital. Name this city.
Santa Fe, New Mexico

179. After the original thirteen colonies, what was the first state to join the union?
Vermont

180. The Chaco Culture National Historic Park is in what US state?
New Mexico

181. The Pine Barrens, a wilderness of bogs, salt marshes, and swamps on the shores of Delaware Bay, is in what US state that has the Kittatinny Mountains to its northwest?
New Jersey

182. The Christa McAuliffe Planetarium, built in honor of the teacher who died in the *Challenger* disaster, is in the city of Concord on the Merrimack River in what US state?
New Hampshire

183. The Alexander Archipelago lies off the coast of what US state?
Alaska

184. The town of Hyde Park, well known as the birthplace of President Franklin D. Roosevelt, is in what US state bordering Lake Champlain and Lake Ontario.
New York

185. What national forest lies near Prince William Sound just south of mountains of the same name as the forest?
Chugach National Forest

186. Name the largest national forest in the United States, which lies in the state of Alaska.
Tongass National Forest

187. The Aleutian islands of Kiska and what other island were the only two islands occupied by the Japanese on the North American continent during World War II?
Attu Island

188. Santa Rosa and Santa Cruz belong to what national park off the coast of California?
Channel Islands National Park

189. The highest peak on the mainland of the United States is in the state of California. Name this peak.
Mt. Whitney

190. Name the national forest in southern Colorado that is named after the mountains that run along the state's southwest.
San Juan National Forest

191. Name the easternmost major Hawaiian city on the Big Island.
Hilo

192. Crater Lake, in Oregon, lies in what mountain range?
Cascade Range

193. What strait separates Vancouver Island from the state of Washington?
Strait of Juan de Fuca

194. In 1803, when Napoleon Bonaparte was the ruler of France, the United States purchased what region from France?
Louisiana Territory

195.   In 1853, the United States purchased a parcel of land along the border with Mexico. This piece of land was known by what name?
Gadsden Purchase

196.   Name the US territory that is part of a chain of islands about 4,800 miles southwest of San Francisco and was formerly known as the Navigator Islands.
American Samoa

197.   In 1917, the United States bought three islands from Denmark. These islands included St. John, St. Croix, and what other island, now part of the US Virgin Islands?
St. Thomas

198.   Name the largest and southernmost island in the Mariana Islands.
Guam

199.   Wake Island, an island north of the Marshalls, is a US possession in what western Pacific island group?
Micronesia

200.   The Northern Marianas are peaks of a huge mountain range that rises from the bottom of the deepest spot in the oceans of the world. Name this spot.
Mariana Trench

201.   Tutuila is the largest island in what American territory in the Pacific?
American Samoa

202.   Charlotte Amalie is a major port in what US territory in the Caribbean?
US Virgin Islands (St. Thomas is acceptable)

203.   A horseshoe-shaped glass walkway, commissioned by the Hualapai Indian tribe, was opened to the public in March 2007. Known as the Grand Canyon Skywalk, this tourist attraction lies along what river?
Colorado River

204. The 2004 G8 summit was held at Sea Island in what US state?
Georgia

205. What fossil fuel provided 90% of the energy consumed in the United States in 1900 but provides only about 22% today?
Coal

206. What country contains 5% of the world's population but uses 26% of the world's oil?
United States

207. As a result of seasonal changes in wind patterns that move fertilizer and other nutrients east from the Mississippi River, harmful "red tides" are blooming along the western coast of what state?
Florida

208. On September 2, 1945, Japan signed the formal surrender papers that brought World War II to an end. This event took place on a famous battleship that served in Desert Storm, World War II, and the Korean War. Name this ship.
USS Missouri

209. What is the only US state that fought for its independence from Mexico?
Texas

210. What act passed by the British parliamentary in 1765 taxed all commercial and legal papers in the American colonies?
The Stamp Act

211. Name the US state that produces more geothermal energy than Iceland.
California

212. High Island is a town in the eastern part of the Bolivar Peninsula in what US state?
Texas

213.   Name the urbanized valley located in the northwestern part of
        Los Angeles.
        San Fernando Valley

214.   In 1508, Ponce de León established Caparra as the first European
        settlement on a U.S. island Commonwealth. Name this island.
        Puerto Rico

215.   Name the only U.S. state divided into parishes.
        Louisiana

216.   Name the U.S. territory about 35 miles west of Haiti's Tiburon
        Peninsula.
        Navassa Island

217.   The Emory River is a stream draining a portion of the
        Cumberland Plateau near Kingston in what state?
        Tennessee

218.   President Rutherford Hayes' birthplace is near the city of Delaware
        in what U.S. state that is home to the Wayne National Forest?
        Ohio

219.   Amicalola Falls State Park is in which US state that has the well
        known J. Strom Thurmond Reservoir on its eastern border?
        Georgia

220.   The Marfa lights, atmospheric reflections of automobile lights, are
        viewed by some as mysterious flashing lights in the night sky and
        are an attraction in the town of Marfa near the Davis Mountains in
        the Chihuahuan Desert of which southwestern state?
        Texas

CHAPTER 2

North America,
Central America,
and the Caribbean

1. The Great Northern Peninsula is the largest and longest peninsula of what Canadian island?
    Newfoundland

2. Tikal in Guatemala and what city in the Mexican state of Chiapas were centers of Mayan civilization?
    Palenque

3. Canada's "cluster of cities," also known as the "golden horseshoe," lies at the western end of what body of water?
    Lake Ontario

4. Name the ancient capital city in Mexico that was built on the island in Lake Texcoco, which is now a small area surrounded by salt marshes.
    Tenochtitlan

5. What Canadian provincial capital city is called the Cradle of Confederation because it was the site of a historic meeting in 1864 that eventually led to the unification of Canada in 1867?
    Charlottetown

6. El Tajin, a pre-Columbian site, is a UNESCO World Heritage Site in the state of Veracruz in what country?
    Mexico

7. What Canadian province shares the Bay of Fundy with Nova Scotia?
    New Brunswick

8. The marshes of Wood Buffalo National Park are, according to some experts, the world's only remaining nesting site for whooping cranes. This is in what Canadian province?
    Alberta

9. Name the three straits that separate Vancouver Island from mainland Canada.
    Johnstone Strait, Queen Charlotte Strait, and the Strait of Georgia

10. Located in the Northwest Territories, what is the longest Canadian river?
    Mackenzie

11. Mt. Logan, Canada's highest peak, is in what Canadian unit?
    Yukon Territory

12. What strait, stretching south from Dixon Entrance, separates the Queen Charlotte Islands from mainland British Columbia?
    Hecate Strait

13. Fort McMurray is a hub for the extraction of bitumen from oil sands. One of the largest exporters of oil to the United States, this site is in what Canadian province?
    Alberta

14. Name the Central American country that borders Honduras and Belize.
    Guatemala

15. A landscape of low hills, lakes, and forests that covers almost half of Canada just south of its Arctic islands is known by what name?
    Canadian Shield

16. The Zapatista National Army, based in the state of Chiapas, has often clashed with the national government of what Latin American country?
    Mexico

17. The North Thompson River, a major tributary of the Fraser River that rises in the Cariboo Mountains, is in what Canadian province?
British Columbia

18. What Caribbean country in the Greater Antilles was originally named Xaymaca by its indigenous Arawakan-speaking Taíno people?
Jamaica

19. Tepic is the capital of which Mexican state?
Nayarit

20. Name the country in the Windward Group that lies 21 miles south of Martinique and 26 miles north of St. Vincent that is sometimes known as the "Helen of the West Indies."
St. Lucia

21. The Bay Islands are one of the eighteen departments of what Central American country whose capital city lies on the Choluteca River?
Honduras

22. The proposed Nicaragua Canal would connect the Caribbean Sea with the Pacific Ocean across a narrow 12-mile-wide land corridor. Name this isthmus.
Isthmus of Rivas

23. The mountain town of Boqueto is on the Baru Volcano in what country that shares La Amistad International Park, a major Central American biosphere reserve, with Costa Rica?
Panama

24.   The Beothuk Indians, also known as the "Red Indians" because of the red painting of their bodies, clothing, and weapons, are the extinct people of what Atlantic Canadian province?
Newfoundland and Labrador

25.   Dinosaur Provincial Park, which contains important fossils dating back to the Age of the Reptiles, is located in the heart of the badlands of what Canadian province?
Alberta

26.   Napoleon III appointed Archduke Maxmillian of Austria to rule what Latin American country from 1832 to 1867?
Mexico

27.   If you are in La P'tit Train du Nord, part of a 124-mile bicycle trail that goes through the Laurentian Mountains, you are in what country in the Western Hemisphere?
Canada

28.   For the Salinan Indians, Morro Rock, a large geological formation off the shore of Morro Bay, is a religious icon. This rock, often called the Gibraltar of the Pacific, is in what country?
USA (in California)

29.   In 1932, Glacier National Park in the United States joined Canada's Waterton Lakes National Park to form the world's first International Peace Park. This park lies in what Canadian province?
Alberta

30.   A festival in Mexico commemorates the 1862 Battle of Puebla, when Benito Juarez defeated French troops. Name this festival.
Cinco de Mayo

31. Until 1815, the Spanish administered the Philippines as a colony of what present-day country?
Mexico

32. The Battle of the Plains of Abraham was fought between the French and the British near what Canadian city?
Quebec City

33. The Ekati diamond mine, located about 124 miles south of the Arctic Circle, is the first diamond mine in Canada. This is in which Canadian territory?
Northwest Territories

34. Name Guatemala's largest department.
Petén

35. On September 25, 1775, an American army general under Richard Montgomery captured what Canadian city?
Montreal

36. Name the 1,240-mile underwater mountain range in the Arctic that has vast oil resources in the North Pole region with conflicting claims by Canada and Russia.
Lomonosov Ridge

37. Buck Island Reef National Monument, one of the few fully marine protected areas in the US National Park system, is in what body of water?
Caribbean Sea (in the Virgin Islands)

38. The Spirit Bear is a black bear that has white fur due to a rare genetic trait. This bear is found mostly in what Canadian province that has the largest island on the western coast of North America?
British Columbia (Vancouver Island)

39.   Many people of African descent in the Caribbean are devotees of a
       religion called Rastafarianism, a religion formed in honor of Haile
       Selassie, the 1930 emperor of what African country that borders
       Djibouti and Kenya?
       Ethiopia

40.   The Klondike River flows near Dawson City in what Canadian
       administrative unit?
       Yukon Territory

41.   Chaco Culture National Historical Park, a UNESCO World
       Heritage Site that includes the Aztec Ruins National Monument,
       lies in what country in North America?
       USA

42.   Name the biggest Pacific island in North America.
       Vancouver Island

43.   Until 1986, Aruba was part of an autonomous dependency of the
       Kingdom of the Netherlands. Name this dependency that was
       dissolved on October 10, 2010.
       Netherlands Antilles
       (Note: Aruba continues to be an autonomous dependency of
       the Kingdom of the Netherlands. On October 10, 2010, the
       Netherlands Antilles were dissolved and some regions (Curacao
       and Sint Maarten) became autonomous territories while Bonaire,
       Saba, and Sint Eustatius became municipalities under the direct
       administration of the Netherlands.)

44.   The Shrine of Saint Lazarus is a holy site in El Rincon in what
       Caribbean country?
       Cuba

45.   Ships passing through the Panama Canal from the Pacific Ocean
       headed for the Atlantic Ocean go in what intermediate direction?
       Northwest

46.　Name the French territory closest to North America.
Saint-Pierre and Miquelon (off Newfoundland)

47.　In 1810, Father Miguel Hidalgo asked hundreds of Indians to rise against Spain in what historic Mexican city?
Dolores

48.　Name the Mexican state that does not belong and explain why: Oaxaca, Chiapas, Guerrero, and Veracruz.
Veracruz, because it is not on the Pacific Coast

49.　Name the northernmost country in Latin America.
Mexico

50.　Which is larger, Turks or Caicos?
Caicos

51.　Manuel Antonio National Park is a wonderful wet tropical forest in the most eco-friendly country in Central America. Name this country.
Costa Rica

52.　Harp seals are an attraction for animal lovers in the Magdalen Islands of Canada. These islands, part of the province of Quebec, lie on what body of water?
Gulf of St. Lawrence

53.　The capital of Belize, in the Cayo District, is named after a river that discharges into the Belize River in this district. Name this river.
Mopan River

54.　The Sarstoon River forms Belize's southern border with what country?
Guatemala

55. The city of Livingstone in Guatemala is home to the descendants of African slaves who escaped Saint Vincent and mixed with the local Carib people. These mixed people are known by what name?
Garifuna

56. Name the Guatemalan city, overlooked by the spectacular Agua Volcano that is widely regarded as one of the best-preserved Spanish colonial cities in the Americas.
Antigua

57. In 2002, the Motagua River Valley in Central America became the site of a green stone rush, a precious stone favored by the Mayans. Name this precious stone.
Jade

58. The state of Tabasco, situated in the northern half of the Isthmus of Tehuantepec and bordered by the Gulf of Campeche to the northeast, is in what country?
Mexico

59. San Pedro Sula is the industrial capital of what Central American country?
Honduras

60. Name the limestone landmass that covers almost all of the northeastern part of Guatemala.
Petén

61. The Lenca people, indigenous to Central America, inhabit El Salvador and what other country on its eastern border?
Honduras

62. An extensive depression that runs across Honduras from the Caribbean to the Pacific Ocean provides a convenient transportation route. What is the name of this valley?
Sula Valley

63. El Mirador is a historic site where the Mayan civilization built some of its largest pyramids. This site is in what present-day country?
Guatemala

64. What is the only non–Central American country that belongs to CAFTA, the Central American Free Trade Agreement?
Dominican Republic

65. The 5,282-foot-tall Concepción Volcano is on the Ometepe Island in what lake in Central America?
Lake Nicaragua

66. La Palma is the capital of Panama's largest, but least populated, province. Name this province.
Darien

67. In 1919, John Alcock and Arthur Whitten-Brown became the first team to fly over an ocean when they flew from the city of St. John's to Ireland. The city of St. John's is in what Canadian province?
Newfoundland and Labrador

68. Low-lying Manabique Peninsula and a portion of the Bay of Amatique form the Caribbean coastline of what Central American country?
Guatemala

69. What northern European religious sect named after Menno Simons, an Anabaptist religious leader from Friesland, has made long-term settlements near the River Hondo in Belize?
Mennonites

70. Name the inlet of the Atlantic Ocean in the Canadian provinces of New Brunswick and Nova Scotia that is known for its marine life and very high tides.
Bay of Fundy

71.   Gros Morne National Park lies on the west coast of Canada's easternmost province. Name this province.
Newfoundland and Labrador

72.   Located south of the Nahanni River, the Nahanni National Park is in what Canadian administrative unit?
Northwest Territories

73.   Grand Etang Lake, which fills the crater of an extinct volcano, is a popular tourist site on a Caribbean island nation just south of Saint Vincent and the Grenadines. Name this country.
Grenada

74.   The Caroni Swamp, at the Asa Wright Nature Center, is one of the best places to see the Scarlet Ibis. This swamp is on an island belonging to a tiny twin-island republic in the Caribbean. Name this island.
Trinidad

75.   In 1534, Jacques Cartier, a French explorer looking for a passage through North America to east Asia, sailed into the Gulf of St. Lawrence and landed on what Canadian peninsula in Quebec?
Gaspe Peninsula

76.   Name British Columbia's longest river.
Fraser River

77.   If you want to see a Turtle Arribada, a mass nesting of turtles, you would travel to what Central American country that has the Guanacaste Cordillera mountain range near its border with Nicaragua?
Costa Rica

78. Guantanamo Bay, where the United States established its naval base and military and interrogation center, lies on which side of Cuba, east or west?
East

79. What French overseas territory in the Caribbean, to the north of Trinidad and Tobago, is often known as the Pearl of the West Indies?
Martinique

80. Puerto Barrios, in the Department of Izabal, served as the only eastern port of a Central American country for almost 100 years. Name this country.
Guatemala

81. Bohio is the former name of what island that is the second-largest and most populous island of the Antilles?
Hispaniola

82. Name the only Caribbean island with a railway system.
Cuba

83. La Fortuna, Costa Rica, was named because it was fortunately spared by what volcano's fury in 1968?
Arenal Volcano

84. In 1821, Limon became independent from Spain. The province of Limon is in what present-day Central American country?
Costa Rica

85. Marble Island, which lies in the northwestern Hudson Bay, is off the coast of what Canadian political unit?
Nunavut

86.   Of the three Latin American civilizations—the Inca, the
      Aztec, and the Maya—one of them did not have a unique
      empire. Instead, they had many warring city-states. Name this
      civilization.
      The Maya

87.   The Thatcher Ferry Bridge, now called the Bridge of the Americas,
      spans which end of the Panama Canal, the Pacific or the Atlantic?
      The Pacific

88.   An island nation lying northwest of the British Overseas Territories
      of Turks and Caicos is considered to be part of the West Indies
      because of its cultural affiliation to the region. Name this nation.
      Bahamas

89.   What island, physically separated from Nova Scotia, celebrates the
      Celtic Colours Festival, an international festival for Scottish, Irish,
      and Acadian traditions, in October of each year?
      Cape Breton

90.   During the Benito Juarez presidency of 1806 to 1872, Mexico was
      able to show a spirited resistance to the occupation of what major
      European power?
      France

91.   Scientists researching the open-sea hideouts of sea turtles have
      often travelled to a site near Great Inagua in what island country
      in the West Indies?
      Bahamas

92.   What coral island in the Lesser Antilles that lies 25 miles north
      of Antigua in the eastern Caribbean Sea, and formerly known as
      Dulcina, has no streams or lakes?
      Barbuda

93.   Name the 365-island archipelago off the northern coast of Panama
        that is called Kuna Yula by the local matriarchal tribes.
        San Blas Islands

94.   Pico Duarte, the highest peak in the Caribbean, is in what country?
        Dominican Republic

95.   On July 22, 1944, delegates from 45 nations voted to create the
        World Bank and the IMF. The conference also promoted the US
        dollar as the standard currency for international transactions.
        These delegates met in what North American city?
        Bretton Woods, New Hampshire, USA

96.   US forces landed on the beaches of Omaha and Utah, renowned
        code names for the historic World War II D-Day landing points.
        What was the code name for the landing site of the Canadian
        forces during this operation?
        Juno Beach

97.   San Lorenzo, Mexico, has a site devoted to what civilization that is
        often regarded as Mexico's first major civilization?
        Olmecs

98.   Copper Canyon provides a wonderful opportunity for nature lovers
        in what Mexican state that borders New Mexico?
        Chihuahua

99.   Mexico's volcanic landscape can be attributed to the meeting of
        four tectonic plates in Mexico. Name them.
        **North American plate, Pacific plate, Cocos plate, and
        Caribbean plate**

100.   Mexico's second-largest city is located on the banks of Lake
        Chapala. Name this city.
        Guadalajara

101.   Madrid, Spain, is on the same latitude as what major city in northeastern United States?
New York City

102.   The Usumacinta River forms the boundary between Mexico and what Central American country?
Guatemala

103.   Sable Island is the only emergent part of the outer Continental Shelf of eastern North America. This island belongs to which Canadian province?
Nova Scotia

104.   Name the small island southwest of Nova Scotia that is connected to the mainland by a causeway over the Barrington Passage.
Cape Sable Island (Cape Island)

105.   Lake Chapala lies on the border of Jalisco and what other Mexican state?
Michoacán

106.   Sisal is a drought-resistant plant named after a port in a Mexican state. Name this state that has Mérida as its capital city.
Yucatán

107.   In 1810, what Mexican priest, who was later honored with a state named after him, called for a rebellion to free Mexico from Spain?
Hidalgo

108.   The famous pyramids of Niches are found in El Tajin, a pre-Columbian archaeological site belonging to what Mexican civilization?
Olmec

109. The Strait of Canso separates the Nova Scotia peninsula from what island?
Cape Breton Island

110. Under what treaty did Mexico gain independence from Spain in 1821?
Treaty of Córdoba

111. Sturgeon is a big draw for fishermen along a 50-mile stretch of what river valley stretching from the town of Mission to Hope in British Columbia, Canada?
Fraser River valley

112. The cities of Cartago and Alajuela are located in what Central American country?
Costa Rica

113. The Miskito Indians, indigenous to Central America, live in a territory that expands from Cape Camarón, Honduras, to Rio Grande in what country along the Mosquito Coast?
Nicaragua

114. The Pugwash Conferences on Science and World Affairs, an international organization that once brought together scholars and public figures to work toward reducing the danger of armed conflicts, was founded in 1957 in what Atlantic Province of Canada?
Nova Scotia

115. What capital in the western Atlantic Ocean is located on New Providence Island?
Nassau

116. Name Canada's second-smallest province by area.
Nova Scotia

117.   The Nelson River, draining into the Hudson Bay, has its source in
       what lake in Canada?
       Lake Winnipeg

118.   The Mosquito Coast that spans Honduras and Nicaragua belonged
       to which European colonial power until 1786?
       Great Britain

119.   Name Nicaragua's highest volcano.
       San Cristobal

120.   Volcano Concepción is on what island in Lake Nicaragua?
       Ometepe Island

121.   A string of volcanoes lines the western edge of Nicaragua all the
       way from the Gulf of Fonseca to what bay on the southwestern
       point of Nicaragua?
       Salinas Bay

122.   What river connects Lake Nicaragua to the Caribbean?
       San Juan River

123.   The Tipitapa River connects Lake Nicaragua with what body of
       water?
       Lake Managua

124.   Name the landlocked Mexican state bordering Veracruz and
       Morelos that has the valley of Tehuacan, considered by some to be
       place where maize was first cultivated by humans.
       Puebla

125.   The small Mayan village church of Santiago Atitlan is on the
       shores of Lake Atitlan in what Latin American country?
       Guatemala

126. Name the most populous country in the Caribbean.
      Cuba

127. The ethnic groups of Creoles, Mestizos, Miskitos, and Garifuna
      form the majority of the population of the city of Bluefields, the
      chief Caribbean port city of what Central American country?
      Nicaragua

128. Name the world's largest uninhabited island, just south of
      Ellesmere Island in Canada.
      Devon Island

129. Zocala Plaza is a place of historical significance in what populated
      city in the Western Hemisphere?
      Mexico City

130. Over the course of the last several years, hurricanes have caused
      destruction in the Granma province of what Caribbean country?
      Cuba

131. Rose Atoll, in Rose Atoll Marine National Monument, is often
      regarded as the southernmost point in the United States. This
      point is in what US territory?
      American Samoa

132. Name Quebec's second largest city, home to the National
      Assembly of Quebec.
      Quebec City

133. Okmok Caldera is located on the island of Umnak. This island,
      one of the Fox Islands, belongs to what larger chain of islands in
      the North Pacific?
      Aleutian Islands

134.   Name the barrier island along Texas' southern Gulf Coast that is connected to the mainland by a causeway from the town of Port Isabel.
South Padre Island

135.   The Fermi National Accelerator Laboratory, or the Fermilab, is located in Batavia in what US state?
Illinois

136.   What country was the first postcolonial independent black nation in the world?
Haiti

137.   What Caribbean nation was the site of the first European settlement in the Americas?
Dominican Republic

138.   What British Overseas Territory is located southeast of the Bahamas and north of Hispaniola?
Turks and Caicos

139.   Choluteca is the southernmost department of Honduras. This department borders what gulf to the west?
Gulf of Fonseca

140.   Name the northern Caribbean country at the junction of the Caribbean Sea, the Gulf of Mexico, and the Atlantic Ocean.
Cuba

141.   What Creole and French speaking country in the Caribbean owns Gonave Island?
Haiti

142. Name the group of islands containing Antigua and Barbuda that makes up the northern end of the Lesser Antilles Chain.
Leeward Islands

143. Name the world's largest island, which is geographically a part of the North American continent.
Greenland

144. Morelia is the capital of Michoacán, which is a state in what Latin American country?
Mexico

145. Dawson Creek is in what Canadian province?
British Columbia

146. Name the North American country that does not have an official language.
USA

147. What country has the world's longest coastline?
Canada

148. What country has the largest lake in Central America?
Nicaragua

149. The Mérida Initiative is a historic program of cooperation between the United States, Mexico, and the countries of Central America for controlling drug trafficking. The city of Mérida is the capital of which Mexican state?
Yucatan

150. Resolute is an Inuit hamlet on a Canadian island just west of Devon Island. Name this island that is part of the Queen Elizabeth Islands.
Cornwallis Island

CHAPTER 3

South America

1. Kangaroos, which belong to the marsupial family, are found
    on the continent of Australia. Opossums, however, also in the
    marsupial family, are found in North America and on what other
    continent?
    South America

2. Lake Titicaca is connected to what other major lake via the
    Desaguadero River in west-central Bolivia?
    Lake Poopo

3. What South American country's name is adopted from the Latin
    word for "silver"?
    Argentina

4. River Pilcomayo forms part of the border between Argentina and
    what other country?
    Paraguay

5. The city of Arica, an important port city in the Atacama Desert, is
    located in what South American country?
    Chile

6. In 2007, a mummy named La Doncella, or the Maiden, made
    headlines in a museum in the provincial capital city of Salta in
    what South American country?
    Argentina

7. The FARC guerillas, near the mountainous Tolima department,
    are a constant source of terrorist threats in the fourth-largest
    country in South America. Name this country.
    Colombia

8. King George Island, the largest island in the South Shetland
    Islands, is claimed by three countries including the southernmost
    country in South America. Name this country.
    Chile

9. São Paulo is the most-populated city in the largest country in South America. Name this country.
Brazil

10. Guayaquil is the largest city in what South American country?
Ecuador

11. Mesopotamia is a region in the northeastern part of which South American country?
Argentina

12. Place the following South American cities in order from north to south: Paramaribo, Georgetown, Cayenne, Caracas.
Caracas, Georgetown, Paramaribo, Cayenne

13. Put the following South American cities in order from south to north: Potosi, La Paz, Asunción (Paraguay), Sucre
Asunción, Potosi, Sucre, La Paz

14. Name the province in Argentina that is named after the Jesuit missionaries who came to spread Christianity to the Guarani people in 1600.
Misiones

15. A stream on Nevado Mismi is considered by many as the most distant source of the Amazon River from its mouth in the Atlantic Ocean. This is in what country bordering Bolivia and Brazil?
Peru

16. Kaieteur Falls, which is five times higher than Niagara Falls, is often considered by many as the largest single drop waterfall in the world. This is in what South American country bordering Suriname?
Guyana

17. If you are cruising through the waters of a South American city with Sugarloaf Mountain looming in the distance, you are in what city?
Rio de Janeiro

18. The city of Ushuaia, located on the island of Tierra del Fuego south of the Strait of Magellan, is the world's southernmost city. This city belongs to what South American country?
Argentina

19. Name the island that does not belong and explain why: San Cristobal Island, Santa Cruz Island, Genovesa (Tower) Island, San Salvador Island.
Genovesa, because it is the only Galapagos Island north of the equator

20. The only hotspot in the world that includes a dry forest ecosystem, despite having abundant rainfall for six months each year, is in Brazil. Name this region.
Cerrado

21. The tallest mountain in South America, Mt. Aconcagua, lies in what province in Argentina?
Mendoza

22. What South American country once had the largest population of British outside of Britain?
Argentina

23. In 1527, Sebastian Cabot, an Italian serving Spain, explored an estuary whose name in Spanish means *Silver River*. Name this estuary.
Rio de la Plata

24. Name the port city about 198 miles north of Buenos Aires alongside the Parana River that is well-known for its late-19th century English and French-style architecture.
Rosario

25. Lakes in the southern part of Argentina could flow either to the Pacific or to the Atlantic due to the fact that they sit directly on top of what physical feature of the earth?
Continental Divide

26. Zoe tribes, known for their seasonal migration, are from what region in South America?
Amazon Rainforest

27. In what South American country do the Yawalapiti tribes live?
Brazil

28. Which is further north, the Falklands or Tierra del Fuego?
Falklands

29. The Atlantic marine reserve of Isla de Lobos is a great place to observe sea lions basking in the sun. This reserve is in what South American country that borders Brazil and Argentina?
Uruguay

30. What is Argentina's northernmost province that borders Chile and Bolivia?
Jujuy

31. Name South America's second longest river.
Paraná River

32. Name the largest freshwater lake between the United States and Peru.
Lake Nicaragua

33. The Casiquiare River connects what river system to the Amazon
     River system?
     Orinoco

34. Mercosur is South America's leading trading bloc. Known as
     the Common Market of the South, it aims to bring about the
     free movement of goods, capital, services, and the people among
     its member states. Mercosur's headquarters is in what city in
     Uruguay?
     Montevideo

35. The northernmost capital city in South America is separated from
     the Caribbean by the steep Avila Mountains. Name this city.
     Caracas

36. In January 2000, a ruptured pipeline spewed about 340,000
     gallons of heavy crude oil into Guanabara Bay in what Brazilian
     city?
     Rio de Janeiro

37. Name Brazil's southernmost state.
     Rio Grande do Sul

38. The equator cuts through what Atlantic Brazilian state that
     borders the state of Para?
     Amapa

39. Porto Velho, capital city of the Brazilian state of Rondonia, grew
     around a port on a tributary of the Amazon River. Name this
     tributary.
     River Madeira

40. The Guiana Highlands border Brazil, Guyana, and what other
     country bordering Colombia?
     Venezuela

41. Name the Brazilian state that does not belong and explain why: Roraima, Mato Grosso, Bahia, Rondonia.
Bahia, because it has a coastline; the others are landlocked

42. What country does not border Argentina: Peru, Chile, Uruguay, Bolivia?
Peru

43. In 1695, gold was discovered in what Brazilian region, which prompted a major population boom, in the southeastern part of the country?
Minas Gerais

44. Name the world's most diverse freshwater ecosystem.
Pantanal

45. In 1763, the Brazilian capital was moved to Rio de Janeiro, from what present-day city, previously known as Bahia?
Salvador

46. The 1822 Battle of Pichincha was fought on the slopes of the Pichincha volcano in what South American country that borders Peru?
Ecuador

47. Mt. Huascaran is situated in the Cordillera Blanca, the world's highest tropical mountain range, in what Andean country?
Peru

48. The world-famous Charles Darwin Research Station is on an island belonging to a group that has Isabela as its largest island. Name this Pacific island group off the coast of South America.
Galapagos

49.   If you are walking in the Urubamba Valley and shopping in Pisac, the marketplace where Quechua Indians sell their handicrafts, you are in what country bordering Ecuador?
        Peru

50.   In 2003, scientists discovered a ninety-million-year-old petrified forest north of the city of Rio Gallegos in what region that is mostly in Argentina and partly in Chile?
        Patagonia

51.   In 1879, British climber Edward Whymper climbed an Ecuadorian summit that is often considered to be the spot farthest from the center of the earth. Name this Andean summit.
        Chimborazo

52.   What city, sometimes known as the Florence of South America, is one of the oldest inhabited cities in the continent and the capital of an empire that once stretched from southern Colombia to central Chile?
        Cuzco

53.   Macumba, which combines African and local religious practices, can be found in a South American country that has Mato Grosso do Sul as its southwestern state. Name this country.
        Brazil

54.   In 1739, Spain transferred responsibility for governing Panama from the viceroyalty of Peru to the viceroyalty of New Granada. What is the present-day name of the country that includes most of the areas covered by the region of New Granada?
        Colombia

55.   Name the capital of the state of Para, in the Amazon delta of Brazil.
        Belem

56. Candomble, an Afro-Brazilian religion that was developed by slaves from Nigeria, has its origins in what popular Nigerian tribe?

Yoruba

57. The 1824 Battle of Ayachucho, where Simón Bolivar defeated the Spanish, gave independence to what South American country that borders Colombia and Bolivia?

Peru

58. The first European visitors to Rapa Nui Islands named them the Easter Islands. These visitors were from what country?

Netherlands

59. The coastal city of Caral, which researchers date to about 2627 B.C.E., is the oldest known city in the Americas. This city on the Pacific coast is in what South American country?

Peru

60. The pre-Incan sacred city of Tiwanacu, in western Bolivia, lies on what body of water?

Lake Titicaca

61. Leatherback turtles are an attraction near the town of Mana in what French department bordering Brazil and Suriname?

French Guiana

62. Whales and dolphins are a major attraction off the coast of Buenaventura in what South American country?

Colombia

63. The Royal Sipan Tombs are located near the city of Chiclayo in what South American country that borders Bolivia and Ecuador?

Peru

64. Emas National Park, near Mineiros, is a great place to glimpse jaguars and tapirs. Mineiros is a small city in the state of Goias in what South American country?
Brazil

65. What historic city in Brazil, just north of Recife, has some of the best examples of 16th- and 17th-century Portuguese architecture?
Olinda

66. According to many, the Manu Biosphere Reserve holds the greatest diversity of life on earth. This protected Amazon ecosystem is situated in what country that borders Brazil?
Peru

67. The Rupununi Savannahs at the foothills of the Pakaraima Mountains is a tropical nature lover's paradise in what South American country that borders Venezuela and Brazil?
Guyana

68. Pinamar, a well-known beach resort, is located just south of the point where River Plate meets the Atlantic Ocean. Pinamar is in what country?
Argentina

69. The lively city of Colonia del Sacramento is a UNESCO World Heritage site in one of the smallest South American republics bounded to the north by Brazil and to the southeast by the Atlantic. This city is in what South American country?
Uruguay

70. Outside of Antarctica, the largest ice fields in the world can be found in what region in South America?
Southern Patagonia

71. Che Guevara, the famous Cuban revolutionary, was born in Rosario in what South American country?
Argentina

72. Capoeira, a martial-arts dance and music, developed by enslaved Africans from Angola, is becoming a cultural landmark of what South American country?
Brazil

73. The city of Cuenca, near the Incan ruins of Ingapirca in Ibarra, is the third-largest city of what South American country?
Ecuador

74. The city of Cochabamba is known as the "City of Eternal Spring" because of its spring-like temperatures all year round. This is the third largest city in what country?
Bolivia

75. The town of Aregua is just east of what city at the confluence of the Paraguay and the Pilcomayo rivers?
Asuncion

76. Name the protected region of Amazon rainforest of Brazil that stretches across international borders and has the Tumuc-Humac Mountains in its upland areas.
Guiana Shield

77. The Putumayo River forms the border of Peru and what other country bordering Brazil?
Colombia

78. What South American country is home to the world's biggest expanse of tropical glaciers?
Peru

79. The Cuyo region in South America consists of the Andean provinces of Mendoza, San Juan, and San Luis and has a unique mestizo population that reflects the influence of Chile. This region is in what country?
Argentina

80. What coastal Chilean city is situated just south of the Tropic of Capricorn?
Antofagasta

81. Talara, the westernmost point in mainland South America, lies in what country?
Peru

82. The northernmost point in mainland South America lies in what country?
Colombia

83. The Paraguay River forms the boundary between Paraguay and what other country besides Argentina?
Brazil

84. Name the three rivers that form the boundary between Paraguay and Argentina.
Paraguay River, Pilcomayo River, and the Paraná River

85. The Paraná River forms the boundary between Paraguay and what other country besides Argentina?
Brazil

86. Place the following cities in order from north to south.
São Paulo, Belo Horizonte, Rio de Janeiro.
Belo Horizonte, Rio de Janeiro, São Paulo

87. Using the equator as a reference, name the city that does not belong in this group and explain why: Belem, Amapa, Manaus, and Porto Alegre.

    Amapa, because it is in the Northern Hemisphere

88. What South American country was formerly known as Dutch Guiana?

    Suriname

89. After reaching the Rio de la Plata, in 1526, Sebastian Cabot, an explorer of Italian descent, sailed up what river that forms the border between Argentina and Paraguay?

    Paraná River

90. Mount Cayambe and Mount Cotopaxi provide crevassed glacial travel adventure for mountaineers in what Andean country?

    Ecuador

91. Name the city that does not belong and why: São Paulo, Recife, Rio de Janiero, La Paz, Lima.

    São Paulo, because it is the only city just south of the Tropic of Capricorn

92. What country that lies entirely in the Northern Hemisphere forms the longest boundary with Brazil?

    Venezuela

93. Name the South American ocean current that does not belong and explain why: Peru Current, Brazil Current, Falkland Current, Cape Horn Current.

    Brazil Current, because it is the only warm current in the group

94.   Name the river that does not belong and explain why: Tapajos,
       Salado, Madeira, Purus.
       **Salado River, because it is a tributary of Colorado River; the
       others are tributaries of the Amazon River**

95.   Other than Barcelona, what Venezuelan city near Caracas has the
       same name as a city in Spain?
       Valencia

96.   The epicenter of the Great Chilean Earthquake in 1960 was near
       what south-central Chilean city just northeast of the coastal town
       of Corral?
       Valdivia

97.   The cities of Cali and Barranquila are in what South American
       country?
       Colombia

98.   Nevado Sajama is the highest peak in what South American
       country?
       Bolivia

99.   The famous Indian village of Otavalo, where shoppers can enjoy a
       variety of handmade goods, is a famous tourist attraction in what
       South American country?
       Ecuador

100.   The 1532 Battle of Cajamarca, where the Spanish captured
       the Incan Emperor Atahualpa, was fought in what present-day
       country?
       Peru

101.   Mount Roraima is the highest point in what South American
       country bordering Brazil?
       Guyana

102. Name the UNESCO World Heritage Site on Colombia's Caribbean coast that is named after a port in the Murcia region of Spain.

     Cartagena

103. What country has the largest proportion of indigenous people in South America and the second-largest reserves of natural gas in the continent?

     Bolivia

104. What South American country is the world's largest producer of copper?

     Chile

105. In the 1930s, Paraguay and Bolivia fought over a vast uninhabited plain that left 100,000 people dead. Name this region.

     Chaco

106. What South American country is credited with the introduction of a dance named the tango?

     Argentina

107. What South American country bordering Venezuela has been fighting a deadly campaign with its left-wing FARC rebels for several years?

     Colombia

108. Ica, a town where scientists found the remains of a large penguin in 2005, is in what country that borders Chile and Ecuador?

     Peru

109. Venezuela and what other South American country have conflicting claims in the timber-rich Essequibo region that spans both the countries?

     Guyana

110. The 1942 Rio Protocol forced Ecuador to relinquish many of its claims in the Amazonian region to what country?
Peru

111. Most Uruguayans are of European origin. They are chiefly from Spain and what other country?
Italy

112. Tarija is a department in which landlocked country once known as Upper Peru during its colonial period?
Bolivia

113. What South American country, where the majority of the people do not speak Spanish, is home to the largest Japanese population outside of Japan?
Brazil

114. The Moquegua region, bordering the regions of Arequipa and Puno, is in what mountainous South American country?
Peru

115. Bovespa, the largest stock exchange in Latin America, is located in what city?
Sao Paulo

116. The Chocó department, which has coastlines on both the Pacific Ocean and the Caribbean, is in what South American country?
Colombia

117. What South American country uses the Real?
Brazil

118. Name the largest city in Peru.
Lima

119. An ancient city belonging to the Wari culture was discovered in what South American country that boasts the second-largest area of tropical forest in South America?

Peru

120. Name the South American country that is the second largest producer of grapes after Italy.

Chile

121. Name the city located at the mouth of the Moche River southwest of the ruins of Chan Chan.

Trujillo

122. Tarija is the southernmost department in which South American country?

Bolivia

123. Monteria is the capital of what Colombian department on the Caribbean?

Córdoba

124. One of the top destinations in South America is located on the border of the Brazilian State of Paraná and the Argentine province of Misiones. Name this tourist destination.

Iguazu Falls

125. The city of Maracay is the entrance to the Henri Pittier National Park, the largest national park in the Cordillera de la Costa region. This is in what South American country on the Caribbean?

Venezuela

CHAPTER 4

Europe

1.   The 1917 Balfour Declaration advocated a homeland for the Jews
     in the Palestine Mandate. This declaration was named after the
     foreign secretary of what country?
     Britain

2.   Name the Italian region that includes the city of Rome.
     Lazio (Latium)

3.   What country does not border Italy—Slovenia, Austria or
     Croatia?
     Croatia

4.   Lower Saxony and Baden-Württemberg are states in what
     European country?
     Germany

5.   The island of Elba is under the jurisdiction of what Italian region?
     Tuscany

6.   Giuseppe Verdi, the leading Italian composer of the 19th century,
     was born in a city in the region of Emilia-Romagna. Today, this
     Etruscan city is well-known for a cheese that is used worldwide.
     Name this city.
     Parma

7.   In 60 C.E., Boudicca, the ancient queen of the Iceni people of
     eastern England, led a historic revolt against what empire that
     occupied most of Britain during that period?
     Roman Empire

8.   Some of the top Alpine ski resorts can be found on the doorstep
     of the largest city in Switzerland. Name this city on the Limmat
     River.
     Zurich

9. What famous 1945 conference, attended by the Soviet Union, the United Kingdom, and the United States, resulted in Masuria becoming part of Poland?
    Potsdam Conference

10. Name the largest lake that is shared by Estonia and Russia.
    Lake Peipus

11. What country is located south of Belarus, northeast of Moldova, and west of Russia?
    Ukraine

12. Name the small Cycladic Island, considered the birthplace of Apollo and Artemis, which lies just west of Míkonos.
    Delos

13. The 11-mile Samariá Gorge, one of the longest gorges in Europe, is located on what island that was the center of Europe's most ancient civilization?
    Crete

14. The Haute Route links Zermatt, Switzerland, with a French town at the foot of Mont Blanc on the Arve River, a tributary of the Rhone. Name this city that was the site of the first Winter Olympics, held in 1924.
    Chamonix

15. Which of these does not belong and why: Basel, Lucerne, Breisach, Antwerp.
    Antwerp, because it is not in the Rhine Basin

16. Which one of these choices does not belong and why: Cologne (Köln), Budapest, Bratislava, and Linz.
    Cologne, because it is on the Rhine, the rest are on the Danube

17. In 1763, France ceded its North American territories to Britain through what famous treaty?
Treaty of Paris

18. In 1215, King John of England was forced to sign what document that limited the powers of the monarch, protected the rights of the citizens, and later influenced many important documents, such as the US Constitution and the Bill of Rights?
Magna Carta

19. In the 1500s, Martin Luther founded the Protestant movement in what European country?
Germany

20. Formed in the year 930 C.E., the Icelandic legislature met regularly at Lögberg, or "Law Rock". Name the settlement where these meetings were held.
Thingvellir

21. The province of Dalarna, home to Lake Siljan, holds one of the largest cross-country ski meets in the world. Dalarna is in the Svealand region of which Scandinavian country?
Sweden

22. The Volga River, the longest river in Europe, is linked by canals to the Baltic Sea, the Black Sea, and another major river in Russia. Name this river.
Don River

23. The Battle of Verdun, one of the costliest battles of World War I, took place in what present-day country?
France

24. The Battle of Thermopylae in 480 B.C.E. was a decisive battle in which a group of city-states was outnumbered when fighting against Persian invaders. The city of Thermopylae is in what present-day country?
Greece

25. On August 26, 1914, Germany defeated Russian forces in the famous Battle of Tannenberg. Tannenberg is in what present-day country?
Poland

26. World War I was fought mostly on land except for one historic naval battle. This battle was fought near what Danish peninsula projecting into the North Sea?
Jutland

27. The five battles of Ypres in World War I were fought in what present-day country?
Belgium

28. The 1917 Battle of Cambrai was well known for its first successful use of tanks. This historic battle was fought in what present-day country?
France

29. Put these cities in order from north to south: Naples, Florence, Rome.
Florence, Rome, Naples

30. Name the Tuscan city, on the banks of the Carrione River, whose quarries produced some of the world's finest white or blue-gray marble used in the construction of the Pantheon and other famous sculptures of the Renaissance.
Carrara

31. Mines in the historic Rhondda Valley of Wales were among the biggest producers of what mineral in the United Kingdom?
Coal

32. The Aegean archipelagos are peaks of submerged mountains with the exception of two volcanic islands. One of them is Mílos. What is the name of the second island, well known for a volcano that destroyed the Minoan city of Akrotiri?
Santorini

33. What is the name of the famous structure built by the ancient Romans across the United Kingdom to protect their empire from the Pictish tribes of Scotland?
Hadrian's Wall

34. The Sava River does not flow through what country—Austria, Slovenia, Croatia, or Bosnia & Herzegovina?
Austria

35. The Sejm is to Poland as the Althing is to what?
Iceland

36. The cities of Banja Luka, Mostar, and Tuzla lie in a country where the Sava River forms part of the boundary with Croatia. Name this country.
Bosnia-Herzegovina

37. The Postojna Cave is a 12-mile labyrinth of subterranean passages created by the Pivka River. This cave is in what country south of Austria?
Slovenia

38. Tartu is a dialect spoken in a country whose second-largest city bears the same name as the dialect. Name this northern European country that borders Russia to its east and Latvia to its south.
Estonia

39. Name the language that is independent of the Indo-European family and commonly spoken by many people in north-central Spain and by some who reside in southwestern France.
Basque

40. The Italian language is based on what dialect, also known as the literary language of Italy?
Tuscan

41. Letzeburgish is spoken in what European country other than France and Germany?
Luxembourg

42. During World War II, the legendary German warship *Bismarck* was sunk by the British near what important naval base on the western tip of Brittany in France?
Brest

43. To see the Kildalton Cross and the Kilnave Cross, both of which date back to about 800 C.E., you would travel to what island off the west coast of Scotland that is the southernmost in the Hebrides?
Isle of Islay

44. St. Andrews, often considered the birthplace of golf, is in what British administrative unit?
Scotland

45. The Rialto Bridge on the Grand Canal, is a popular tourist destination in what European city?
Venice

46. The historic ruins of Butrint lie on a small peninsula between the Straits of Corfu and Lake Butrint. These ruins, overlooking the Vivari Channel, are found in what European country?
Albania

47.   Sambre-Meuse Valley divides a country bordering Luxembourg
       into two distinct physical and cultural regions. Name this
       country.
       Belgium

48.   What is the name of the canal in the Kempenland region of
       Belgium that links the Meuse and the Schelde Rivers and carries
       barge traffic on the way to Antwerp?
       Albert Canal

49.   What medieval city, a UNESCO World Heritage Site, is the
       capital of the Belgian province of West Flanders?
       Bruges

50.   In the 1713 Treaty of Utrecht, France released its claim to the
       region known as Spanish Netherlands. What is the present-day
       name of the country that comprises this region?
       Belgium

51.   The Battle of the Golden Spurs is a major celebration for what
       ethnic group in Belgium?
       Flemish

52.   What is the name of the Belgian province that shares its name
       with a neighboring country?
       Luxembourg

53.   Name the river that forms part of the border between the
       Netherlands and Belgium and is known by different names in the
       two countries.
       Maas (Netherlands) or Meuse (Belgium)

54.   Name the city in the Netherlands, the site of a famous World War
       II battle, which lies at the confluence of the Rhine, IJssel, and
       Waal Rivers.
       Arnhem

55. What is the name of the Germanic people who descended from the Frisians, the Saxons, and the Franks?
Dutch

56. What is the name of the famous bridge over the Rhine that helped the Allies isolate the Germans in the "Bridge Too Far" Operation during World War II?
Arnhem Bridge

57. The Zuiderzee, an inlet of the North Sea, was closed off in 1932 by a long dike, forming what freshwater lake, the largest in Western Europe?
IJsselmeer

58. The Elfstedentocht, a long-distance skating race across eleven cities, is held in what northern province in the Netherlands?
Friesland

59. What city in the Netherlands is the home to the Anne Frank museum?
Amsterdam

60. The Netherlands' highest point, Vaalser Berg in the Southern Uplands region, is near what industrial city where the Treaty on European Union was signed on February 7, 1992?
Maastricht

61. The Murcia region is one of the least developed regions in what country on the Iberian Peninsula?
Spain

62. The Palio horse race, held in the Piazza del Campo, is one of the biggest events held in what Tuscan city?
Siena

63.   Name the alliance in effect between the 13th and the 17th centuries
        that helped maintain a trade monopoly over the Baltic Sea, the
        North Sea, and most of northern Europe that included the Baltic
        towns of Danzig and Lübeck.
        Hanseatic League
        (Note: it also provided security from pirates)

64.   In 793 C.E., the Viking raiders set sail from Jutland, Denmark,
        to a tidal island off the northeast coast of England. This island is
        now connected to the mainland of Northumberland by a causeway
        on the English coast. Name this historic island.
        Lindisfarne

65.   Dogfights in the sky destroyed Germany's air superiority in what
        famous World War II battle in 1940 that is often regarded as the
        first major battle fought entirely by air forces?
        Battle of Britain

66.   In 1859, four years before publishing his first novel, *Five Weeks
        in a Balloon,* Jules Verne moved to the Latin Quarter of what
        European capital city that is a tourist haven and houses many
        educational institutions and restaurants?
        Paris

67.   The Rion-Antirion Bridge is built across what body of water in
        Greece's earthquake zone?
        Gulf of Corinth

68.   Muslims under the leadership of Saladin, a 12th-century military
        leader, were engaged in religious wars with Christian kingdoms.
        These wars are known in history by what name?
        Crusades

69.   In June every year, the island of Hydra celebrates the Miaoulia
        festival. This island belongs to what European country?
        Greece

70. The medieval city of Kotor in the Adriatic is a major tourist center in what country in southeastern Europe?
Montenegro

71. During the Middle Ages, non-Catholics were forced to settle in what is now Northern Ireland in the region of Ulster. These Ulster Irish were originally from what division of the present-day United Kingdom?
Scotland

72. The largest city north of the Arctic Circle is in European Russia. Name this city.
Murmansk

73. Name the administrative center of the Pitcairn Islands, a United Kingdom territory.
Adamstown

74. What European capital city lies on the Alzette and Pétrusse rivers?
Luxembourg

75. Marshal Tito, president of the former Yugoslavia, was born in Kumrovec in what present-day country that has the well-known Old City of Dubrovnik and Diocletian's Palace in the city of Split?
Croatia

76. What country on the Adriatic, whose name means "black mountain", uses the Euro but is not part of the European Union?
Montenegro

77. Many gypsies, also known as the Roma, live in what country that has the historic Moravian Gate, a traditional military corridor between the North European Plain and the Danube in central Europe?
Czech Republic

78. Well known for its Tours Cathedral and the famous Chateaux of the Loire Valley, this region of France has Orleans as its capital city. Name this region.
Centre

79. Žabljak, near the Tara River Canyon, is an important tourist spot in what European country?
Montenegro

80. The ancient monument of Agora, which served as a marketplace and a forum during its glory days, is located in what European country?
Greece

81. Between 1789 and 1799, France's society and political system underwent major transformations. This period is known to historians by what name?
French Revolution

82. The Battle of the Bulge was fought in what European forest region that lies in Belgium, Luxembourg, and France?
Ardennes

83. Name the holy mountain where Eastern Orthodox monasteries form a self-governing state on a peninsula in Macedonia, Greece.
Mount Athos

84. The Cathedral of Chartres, one of the finest examples of Gothic style architecture, is located about 50 miles southeast of what European capital city?
Paris

85. The Black Sea warriors of the Middle Ages, who once lived in Greece, Turkey, and Bulgaria and were known for their mystery gold, are known by what popular name in the historical chronicles?
Thracians

86. Vulcano and Lipari are the southernmost islands of what Italian archipelago?

Aeolian archipelago

87. In 2006, a 27,000-year-old human skeleton was discovered in a cave in the Vilhonneur forest in the department of Charente, an administrative unit named after the Charente River, in what country?

France

88. Windsor Castle, one of the largest and oldest inhabited castles in the world, is in what country?

United Kingdom

89. The ancient Roman city of Ostia lies at the mouth of what river?

Tiber River

90. Where is the Saint-Rémy asylum, where artist Vincent van Gogh produced *Wild Vegetation*?

Provence, France

91. The Rhone Glacier, the source of a major European river of the same name, is in what European country?

Switzerland

92. The high-speed TGV train connects Paris with the capital of the French region of Rhône-Alpes. Name this city.

Lyon

93. After WWI and the dissolution of the Ottoman Empire, Iraq came under the rule of what European power?

Great Britain

94.   The town of Orange, renowned for the best-preserved Roman theatre
        in Europe, was listed in 1981 as a UNESCO World Heritage Site.
        This town is in the department of Vaucluse in what country that was
        one of the founding members of the European Union?
        France

95.   Lake Saimaa is located in what European country?
        Finland

96.   Name the river that forms part of the border between Lithuania
        and the Kaliningrad oblast of Russia.
        Neman River

97.   What strait separates Sicily from Calabria?
        Strait of Messina

98.   The city of Zaragoza is on Spain's longest river that has its source
        in Cantabria. Name this river.
        Ebro River

99.   The historic city of Dunkirk is in what country?
        France

100.   The Fens, a natural region of about 15,500 square miles of
        reclaimed marshland, are in the eastern part of what British
        administrative unit?
        England

101.   The city of Katowice is located in the southern part of what
        country?
        Poland

102.   The region of Moravia is in what country bordering Austria?
        Czech Republic

103. The island of Chios belongs to what country in the Mediterranean Sea?
Greece

104. Name the country located east of Lake Ohrid.
Macedonia

105. Name the city that does not belong and explain why: Bratislava, Novi Sad, Stuttgart, Gyor.
Stuttgart, because it is not on the Danube River

106. What westernmost capital city in Europe lies in the historic province of Estremadura, Portugal?
Lisbon

107. Vindobona was a Celtic settlement that later became a Roman military camp on the site of what modern European city?
Vienna

108. Name the city that was the medieval capital of Spain and home of the famous painter El Greco in 1577.
Toledo

109. Mezquita, the world-famous Great Mosque that was begun by Moors in 785 C.E., demonstrates the beauty of Islamic architecture. This is in what Spanish city?
Córdoba

110. Name the historical region in eastern Czech Republic that takes its name from the river that rises in its northwest.
Moravia

111. What is the largest island in the Baltic Sea, which is well known for Viking treasure and a walled medieval city?
Gotland

112.   Longboats were a feature of what fierce warrior culture that
        terrorized Europe from the late 700s to about 1100 C.E.?
        Vikings

113.   It is not uncommon to find King Penguins on a sub-Antarctic
        archipelago of small islands in the southern Indian Ocean. Name
        this island group, which is part of the French Southern Territories.
        Crozet Islands

114.   The port city of Piraeus in Greece is located on what gulf?
        Saronic Gulf

115.   The Donets Basin, a region rich in coal, is located in what
        European country that borders Moldova and Romania?
        Ukraine

116.   Rennes is the capital city of what region of France?
        Brittany

117.   The megaliths at Carnac, on the Morbihan Coast, is one of the oldest
        megalithic sites found in Europe. This site is in what country?
        France

118.   During World War II, the government of what country built the
        Atlantic Wall, a defensive fortification, along the western coast of
        Europe?
        Germany

119.   The Foloi Plateau is located in the Ileia prefecture of what
        European country?
        Greece

120.   What Spanish city is home to the well-known Prado Museum?
        Madrid

121. The Pergamon Museum, which was badly damaged during World War II, is in what European city?
Berlin

122. The Ebro, Spain's major river, rises in what mountains before flowing into the Mediterranean Sea?
Cantabrian Mountains

123. In 2007, archaeologists discovered neolithic spears, amber jewelry, and 500-year-old gum in Oulu—which, in the Sami language, means "floodwater"—in the Northern Ostrobothnia region of what European country?
Finland

124. Name the Spanish city on the Guadalquivir River that is the cultural capital of southern Spain and has the well-known Moorish palace, the Alcázar.
Seville

125. The Medicis, an influential family that produced three popes from the 13th to the 17th century, were from what Italian city?
Florence

126. The famous Battle of Alcoy was fought between the Moors and the Christians in what Spanish region?
Valencia

127. The Battle of Chalons, fought in 451 C.E. between the Romans and Visigoths against the Huns, was the last major military operation of the western Roman Empire. Chalons is in what present-day country?
France

128. The Second Punic War was fought in Cannae near Apulia on the Adriatic coast. Cannae is in what present-day European country?
Italy

129.   Physicist Gabriel Fahrenheit, who developed the temperature
       scale, hails from what country?
       Germany

130.   The naval Battle of Vigo Bay was fought during the War of the
       Spanish Succession between the Anglo-Dutch and a French-
       Spanish fleet. Vigo Bay is in what northwestern autonomous
       community of Spain?
       Galicia

131.   Oviedo is the capital of the principality of Asturias in what
       European country?
       Spain

132.   What famous European river originates in the southern Massif Central,
       flows north, and then west before entering the Atlantic Ocean?
       Loire

133.   What Spanish provincial capital lies near the Llobregat and Besos
       rivers?
       Barcelona

134.   If you are walking in Lauterbrunnen, a town in the shadow of the
       jagged peaks of a mountain range in Switzerland, you are near
       what specific Alpine range?
       Bernese Alps

135.   The island of Kizhi is an open-air museum of wooden architecture
       that highlights the traditional culture of the aboriginal peoples in
       the Karelia republic of what country that borders the Baltic Sea?
       Russia

136.   The medieval market town of Tewkesbury is located near the
       confluence of the River Avon and what other major river, Britain's
       longest?
       River Severn

137. What mountains lie just east of Aberdeen, Scotland?
Grampian Highlands

138. Charles Bridge, along which statues of saints have been positioned, has helped to make what European capital a hot tourist spot?
Prague

139. In 1975, President Ford signed an agreement in a European capital city that ratified borders in Soviet-dominated Eastern Europe. Name this accord.
Helsinki Accords

140. The island of Diego Garcia, controlled by the United Kingdom, belongs to what archipelago in the Indian Ocean?
Chagos Archipelago

141. The Dom Tower in the Netherlands is located in what modern-day city that was once known as the ancient Roman city of Traiectum?
Utrecht

142. Waterloo, site of the famous battle fought by Napoleon, is in what country?
Belgium

143. According to reports, which country has the most reported tornado events of any European nation?
United Kingdom

144. Flores Island is the westernmost island in what European-controlled archipelago about 2,400 miles east of North America?
Azores

145. The Oresund Bridge, which is the longest combined road-and-rail bridge in Europe, connects Copenhagen and the city of Malmo. Malmo is the third-largest city in what country?
Sweden

146. Kavala is the largest seaport in the Eastern Macedonian region of what country?
Greece

147. Most of the world's cork comes from the Alentejo region of what European country?
Portugal

148. A Polish city that has Old Town as a UNESCO World Heritage Site is one of the cities that was spared from heavy bombings during World War II. Name this city.
Krakow

149. Name the largest lake in Hungary.
Lake Balaton

150. The World War II Battle of Anzio was fought in what European country?
Italy

151. The town of Oswiecim, Poland, is on what river?
Vistula River

152. The island of La Gomera, where Columbus stayed as his ships replenished supplies, is part of what island group in the Atlantic that used to be called the Fortunate Islands?
Canary Islands

153. A European country supplies gas to Great Britain via the longest underwater pipe in the world. Name this country.
Norway

154. The Saxons fortified their towns against Darius with castles called burhs. One of these stone castles can be found in Dover on the southeast coast of what country?
United Kingdom

155. Which country is European Union's leading import partner?
China

156. Gibraltar was once part of what medieval kingdom in Spain?
Granada

157. Name the Spanish town originally founded by the Romans and later fortified with town walls by Christians who lived in the 11th-century kingdom of Castile.
Avila

158. Normans built a castle in Rochester, Kent, after the Battle of Hastings in what present-day country?
United Kingdom

159. What channel separates the island of Ireland from Great Britain?
St. George's Channel

160. What city, famous for cloth making and known as a major port in 13th-century Tuscany, was built on a flat plain on both sides of the River Arno?
Florence

161. The shrine of St. James the Greater is a holy site at Compostela in what Spanish region?
Galicia

162. The famous Bayeux tapestry is an account of the successful 1066 Norman invasion of what present-day political unit in the United Kingdom?
England

163. Johannes Gutenberg invented the mechanical printing press and was the first to use movable type printing in Europe. Gutenberg was born in the town of Mainz in what country?
Germany

164. The provinces of A Coruña, Lugo, Ourense, and Pontevedra make up what region in the northwestern corner of Spain?
Galicia

165. During the Middle Ages, Emperor Augustus enlarged the port of Ravenna in the northeastern part of what European country?
Italy

166. In the post–World War II breakup of the Austro-Hungarian Empire, which province of Hungary became a part of Austria with its provincial capital at Eisenstadt?
Burgenland

167. The largest city in Germany's Rhine-Ruhr metropolitan area is home to Europe's largest cathedral. Name this city, which was spared by Allied bombing during World War II.
Cologne

168. The Thirty Years' War, between 1618 and 1648, was fought primarily in what present-day European country?
Germany

169. Münster, a city in the westernmost German state, was the site of the Treaty of Westphalia, which ended the Thirty Years' War in 1648. Name this state.
North Rhine-Westphalia

170. The 1919 Treaty of Versailles, which ended World War I, was signed by the Allies, the Associated Powers, and Germany. Versailles is a suburb of what French city?
Paris

171. Name the river, known to the Arabs as the "Great River," that passes through the olive groves of Jaén and the fruit orchards of Córdoba in Spain.
Guadalquivir River

172. One of the largest cities in Spain is the capital of Andalusia. Name this city.
Seville

173. Pico de Teide, the highest point in Spain, is on what island?
Tenerife

174. Doñana National Park, one of the most important European refuges for wild animals, lies on the estuary of what river?
Guadalquivir River

175. What Spanish region borders Andorra?
Catalonia

176. What is the largest of the Balearic Islands?
Majorca

177. *Guernica* is a painting by Pablo Picasso depicting the Nazi German bombing of the town by the same name. Guernica is in what autonomous Spanish region that houses the famous Bilbao Museum?
Basque Provinces

178. The bullring in Ronda is considered one of the oldest in Spain. Ronda is in what Spanish region?
Andalusia

179. Name the Muslim fortress complex that is a UNESCO World Heritage Site overlooking the city of Granada, Andalusia.
Alhambra

180.   The Severn, United Kingdom's longest river, discharges into what channel?
       Bristol Channel

181.   Name the famous British tourist district known for its magnificent hilly regions lying to the north of Lancashire in northwest England.
       Lake District

182.   The German stock exchange and the European Central Bank are situated in what city on the Main River?
       Frankfurt

183.   Name Britain's second-largest city.
       Birmingham

184.   The counties of Essex, Suffolk, Norfolk, and Cambridgeshire make up what British region?
       East Anglia

185.   The Buttermere Valley, one of the remote areas in the Lake District, is in what English county?
       Cumbria

186.   The capital city of Wales is located in southern Wales on the Bristol Channel. Name this city that in 1794 became an important port for transporting coal from the Welsh coalfields.
       Cardiff

187.   After London, what is the United Kingdom's largest port?
       Liverpool

188.   Beethoven was born in the former West German capital city. Name this city.
       Bonn

189. Name one of the greatest monuments of ancient Britain in Wiltshire, located on the Salisbury Plain in southwest England.
Stonehenge

190. Name the northernmost British city that is served by British Railways, which lies where the River Ness meets the Moray Firth, an inlet of the North Sea.
Inverness

191. The 600 years in Europe that followed the fall of the Roman Empire in 476 C.E. has often been known by what name?
Dark Ages (also known as Early Middle Ages)

192. Johann Sebastian Bach was born in Eisenach, a city in the state of Thuringia. During the Cold War, Thuringia was part of the Eastern bloc of this divided country. Name this present-day reunified country.
Germany

193. What Germanic people settled on the island of Great Britain in the 5th century?
Anglo-Saxons

194. The Dnieper River, which originates in the Valdai Hills of Russia, runs through what countries before emptying into the Black Sea?
Belarus and Ukraine

195. After the Russian Revolution, Lenin signed the Brest Treaty in which Russia ceded the Baltic regions, parts of Ukraine, and Belarus to a country, ending the war between Russia and that country. Name that country.
Germany

196. The headquarters of OPEC, an international cartel of oil-producing nations, is in what European city?
Vienna

197.   The Diet (parliament of Japan) is to Japan as Bundestag is to
        what?
        Germany

198.   What is Greece's second-largest city?
        Thessaloniki

199.   On August 19, 1942, the World War II Battle of Dieppe was
        fought between the Allies and German forces in what country?
        France

200.   The legendary hiding place of Robin Hood, Sherwood Forest,
        which once covered about 100,000 acres, is now reduced to a
        mere 450 acres. This forest is in the East Midlands region of what
        present-day English county?
        Nottinghamshire

201.   The European Court of Human Rights is headquartered in the
        city of Strasbourg in what country?
        France

202.   In December 1992, a Greek-flagged tanker named the *Aegean Sea*
        spilled 80,000 tons of crude oil near the port of A Coruña in what
        European country?
        Spain

203.   The House of Juliet (Casa di Giulietta), a 13th-century home in
        an Italian city on the Adige River in the Po Valley, is believed to
        have inspired Shakespeare's *Romeo and Juliet.* Name this city.
        Verona

204.   Leipzig and Dresden are cities in the German state of Saxony.
        Saxony borders Poland and what other country?
        Czech Republic

205. Name the large four-fingered peninsula south of the Gulf of Corinth in southern Greece.
Peloponnese

206. Europort, the largest human-made harbor port complex, east of the Hook of Holland, is in what city?
Rotterdam

207. The River Clyde runs through one of the most populous cities in the United Kingdom whose name means the "dear green place" in the Gaelic language. Name this west central Scottish city.
Glasgow

208. Many ancient Greek cities were built on hills with steep sides to protect them from invaders. This fortified high area of a city is known by what Greek term?
Acropolis

209. Balti, on the Raut River, is an important railway junction in which landlocked European country?
Moldova

210. The FTSE Index is to the United Kingdom as DAX is to what?
Germany (CAC is to France)

211. What northern Belgian plateau bordering the Netherlands, between the Scheldt and the Meuse rivers, is a major mining and industrial center?
Kempenland

212. Delft, famous for its blue and white pottery called Delftware, is a city in what European country?
Netherlands

213. Flanders is to Dutch as Wallonia is to what?
French

214.   The inhabitants of what northern Netherlands province speak a
        dialect that is closer to old English than Dutch?
        Friesland

215.   The Rijksmuseum in the Netherlands houses works of art by
        Flemish, Dutch, Italian, and Spanish masters from the 15th to 19th
        centuries. This museum is in what city on the North Sea Canal in
        the North Holland province?
        Amsterdam

216.   In 1830, the province of North Brabant was established to
        separate it from its southern counterpart in present-day Belgium.
        North Brabant is a province in what country?
        Netherlands

217.   The oldest university in the Netherlands was founded in a city in
        South Holland that lies at the confluence of the Old Rhine and
        the New Rhine rivers. Name this city that is situated about 10
        miles northeast of The Hague and 5 miles inland from the
        North Sea.
        Leiden

218.   The city of Frankfurt is in what German state?
        Hesse

219.   Patmos is the northernmost island in what Greek island group?
        Dodecanese

220.   Name the largest of the Dodecanese Islands in Greece.
        Rhodes

221.   Name the Greek island that does not belong and explain why:
        Milos, Santorini, Corfu, Naxos.
        **Corfu, because it is not part of the Cyclades; it is part of the
        Ionian Islands**

222. Brenner Pass connects Austria to Italy through the Alps. This pass is in an Austrian region that extends into Italy and was often a disputed area in the past. Name this region.
Tirol

223. Europe's largest ancient Celtic settlement, found at Magdalensberg, is in what Austrian state that borders Italy and Slovenia?
Carinthia

224. The Mediterranean region named the French Riviera is off the coast of Monaco and what French region that borders Monaco?
Provence

225. The French region of Aquitaine borders what body of water?
Bay of Biscay

226. The French city of Lyon lies at the confluence of the Saone and what other river that empties into the Gulf of Lion?
Rhone River

227. What country borders the French region of Midi-Pyrenees and Spain?
Andorra

228. Name the southernmost major port on the Gulf of Finland.
Tallinn

229. The ancient city of Pskov, Russia, is on the Velikaya River. This river drains into what lake just west of the city?
Lake Peipus

230. What is the most-populated German state?
North Rhine-Westphalia

231. Put the following islands in order, from north to south: Isle of
      Man, Orkney Islands, Outer Hebrides, Inner Hebrides.
      Orkney Islands, Outer Hebrides, Inner Hebrides, Isle of Man

232. The Welsh town of Swansea lies on what channel?
      Bristol Channel

233. What hills form the border between Scotland and England?
      Cheviot Hills

234. Six million pilgrims visit a site in France that has a reputation for
      miracle healings. Name this city situated in the southwest of the
      Hautes-Pyrénées department in southern France.
      Lourdes

235. Bouvet Island and Peter I Island are Norway's overseas territories
      off the coast of what continent?
      Antarctica

236. An island that lies northwest of the French city of Rennes, off the
      coast of Lower Normandy, was fortified in 1256 and resisted sieges
      during the Hundred Years' War and the French Wars of Religion.
      Name this island.
      Mont-Saint-Michel

237. Name the small island to Iceland's northeast located between the
      Greenland Sea and the Norwegian Sea that is often identified with
      the location of the northernmost active volcano on earth.
      Jan Mayen

238. The Parc Astérix, an entertainment theme park that attracts
      families from all over France, was inspired by a French comic book
      hero named Asterix the Gaul. This park is located 19 miles north
      of what French city?
      Paris

239. The landmark clock tower in Styria's state capital, unlike other clocks, tells the hour by its long hand and the minute by its short hand. Name this Austrian city.

Graz

240. In 1908, a 4.4-inch limestone statue of historical significance was discovered in the Wachau Valley of what European country?

Austria

241. Charles Lindbergh completed the first solo trans-Atlantic flight in 1927, traveling nonstop from the United States to what European country?

France

242. Mount Pendeli, north of what European capital city, provided quarries and building material for its ancient monuments?

Athens

243. Puffins are a wonderful sight for bird lovers on the Treshnish Isles in what administrative unit of the United Kingdom?

Scotland

244. Piccadilly Circus, a famous road junction and home to the legendary statue of Eros, is in what European capital city?

London

245. Name Norway's second-largest city after Oslo.

Bergen

246. The mythical god Boreas is believed to have brought the cold north winds to a European city in the Hellenic Republic. The "Tower of the Winds," a marble structure built in his honor is now a major tourist attraction in this city. Name this city.

Athens

247.   In a Greek epic poem, a fierce battle involving a woman, a
        boy named Paris, and the gods of Olympus was fought in the
        city of Ilium. This city, once part of ancient Greece, is now an
        archaeological site in Turkey. What is another name for this site?
        Troy

248.   The city of Toulouse, nestled among the Pyrenees approximately
        450 miles from Paris, lies along what river?
        Garonne River

249.   Name Finland's main Baltic Sea port, which is also its third-
        largest city.
        Turku

250.   The second-largest city in Austria lies along the Mur River in the
        southeastern part of the country. Name this city.
        Graz

251.   Name the autonomous Finnish island group, at the entrance of
        the Gulf of Bothnia, which has Swedish as an official language and
        Mariehamn as the capital city.
        Aland Islands

252.   In 1618, the Protestant state of Bohemia revolted against the
        Catholic alliance led by German emperor Ferdinand II. The
        Bohemian revolt led to a war that involved several European
        countries that ultimately ended with the 1648 Peace of
        Westphalia. In history, this war is known by what popular name?
        Thirty Years' War

253.   The Appian Way, Italy's most important ancient Roman road,
        connected Rome to what city in the region of Puglia (or Apulia)
        at the heel of the Italian boot?
        Brindisi

254. Sirnak is a province in the southeastern Anatolian region of what country bordering Iraq and Bulgaria?
Turkey

255. In May 1949, the Soviet Union lifted its failed blockade of what European city following a counter-offensive airlift of supplies by the United States and Great Britain?
Berlin

256. Name the only Baltic state that does not border Belarus.
Estonia

257. Trench warfare is often associated with which world war?
World War I

258. Nobel Prize winner Lech Walesa, who organized the trade union known as Solidarity, became the first freely elected president of what European country?
Poland

259. Frisian is the official language of Frisia, a province in what country in northwestern Europe?
Netherlands

260. Mt. Hekla is the most active volcano in what European country?
Iceland

261. Name Latvia's largest river in terms of volume.
Daugava River

262. Name the heavily fortified zone that ran from Lens to Verdun, near the border of France and Belgium, which the Allies were able to break through in 1918.
Hindenburg Line (or Siegfried Line, as was known to Germans)

263. In 1939, Germany and the Soviet Union agreed to divide control of occupied Poland roughly along what river that now forms a portion of the border between Poland and Ukraine?
Bug River

264. Linz, a leading cultural center that has a Roman castle-settlement from the 1ˢᵗ century C.E., is in what European country?
Austria

265. In the last days of the Roman Empire, this city was the capital of Gaul and was known as "Little Rome." Name this city that has the same name as a zodiac sign.
Aries

266. Of the following German cities, name the city that does not belong in the group and explain why: Dresden, Meissen, Prague, and Mannheim.
Mannheim, because it is on Rhine River; the rest are on the Elbe River

267. A French city on the Rhone River is known as the "City of Popes" due to the role the city played when the popes lived in the area for much of the 14ᵗʰ century. Name this city.
Avignon

268. Trieste is a major city in the northeastern part of a country that borders Slovenia and France. Name this country.
Italy

269. Name the only island that belongs to Iceland that lies on the Arctic Circle.
Grimsey Island

270. Hans Christian Andersen was born in Denmark's third-largest city. Name this city on Funen (Fyn), Denmark's third-largest island.
Odense

271. Prehistoric menhirs, rocklike structures left behind by ancient pre-Celtic people who once inhabited the area, are located in what coastal town in Brittany?
Carnac

272. Lake Como is in the Lombardy region of what country bordering Switzerland?
Italy

273. Euskara, a language borrowed from French, Latin, and Spanish, is spoken by what ethnic group in France?
Basques

274. Stuttgart is the capital of what German state?
Baden-Württemberg

275. "Hexagon" is a nickname used by the locals of a European country bordering Germany to refer to their own nation. Name this country.
France

276. Impressionist Claude Monet's garden in Giverny is an important site for art lovers visiting what European country?
France

277. What term is used by historians to describe the short-lived democratic period in Germany from 1919 to 1933?
Weimar Republic

278. The Republic of Kalmykia is home to the only traditionally Buddhist population in Europe. This republic is in what country?
Russia

279. Denmark's southernmost point is on what island off the Baltic Sea coast?
Falster

280.   The Evros River forms part of the boundary between Greece and
       what other country?
       Turkey

281.   Name Denmark's largest island outside of Greenland.
       Zealand (Sjaelland)

282.   Russia borders what two European countries via the Kaliningrad
       oblast?
       Poland and Lithuania

283.   The Gulf of Genoa is an extension of what sea?
       Ligurian Sea

284.   Europe's only desert, the Tabernas Desert, is in what country?
       Spain

285.   Name the Portuguese archipelago in the Atlantic, about 2,400
       miles east of North America.
       Azores

286.   Victor Hugo, who wrote *The Hunchback of Notre Dame* and *Les
       Misérables,* hails from what European country?
       France

287.   Pompeii, in the Campania region of Italy, is closest to what major
       coastal city?
       Naples

288.   In 1240 C.E., the Mongols destroyed what east Slavic state
       dominated by the city of Kiev?
       Kievan Rus

289.   What country is often considered to have the world's oldest
       parliamentary democracy?
       Iceland

290. Name Latvia's longest river.
Guaja River

291. The Cotentin Peninsula (also known as Cherbourg Peninsula) belongs to what country that is situated to the east of the Channel Islands?
France

292. Name the limestone plateau region of southwestern Slovenia that extends into northeastern Italy.
Kras Plateau

293. The Italian regions of Emilia-Romagna and Marches, on the Adriatic coast, border what European country?
San Marino

294. Campania region of what European country borders the Tyrrhenian Sea to its west.
Italy

295. What is the country whose border with Moldova is formed in part by the Prut River?
Romania

296. What European country has the Bay of Kotor in its southwestern region on the Adriatic Sea?
Montenegro

297. The Schengen Agreement allows for a waiver of cross-border passport checks. This agreement is named after the town of Schengen, situated where the borders of Germany, France, and Luxembourg meet. Schengen belongs to what country?
Luxembourg

298.   The British crown dependency of Sark belongs to a group of
       islands off the French coast of Normandy. Name this island group.
       Channel Islands

299.   Name the largest city on Europe's Attica Peninsula that juts into
       the Aegean Sea.
       Athens

300.   Name the European country that is well known for the profusion
       of coal in its northeastern Masuria region.
       Poland

301.   The Italian island of Lampedusa, on the Mediterranean, belongs to
       what group of islands located between Malta and Tunisia, south of
       Sicily?
       Pelagian Islands

302.   The Crimean city of Yevpatoria is located in the largest country
       that is situated entirely within Europe. Name this country.
       Ukraine

303.   Name the largest city in the Basque Country of Spain.
       Bilbao

304.   Gazprom, the Russian government's gas monopoly, supplies
       natural gas to what country that has Odesa as the largest city
       along the Black Sea?
       Ukraine

305.   Name the northwestern non-NATO European country on the
       Celtic Sea that belongs to the EU.
       Republic of Ireland

306.   Devon is a county in the United Kingdom that has its northern
        coastline on the Bristol Channel. This county is in what political
        unit of the United Kingdom?
        England

307.   Innsbruck is in what Austrian federal province that is part of a
        historical region that extends into southern Italy?
        Tirol

308.   Name the country whose largest city is Podgorica.
        Montenegro

309.   What European country is officially known as the Hellenic
        Republic?
        Greece

310.   Which Nordic country is the largest country in northern Europe?
        Sweden

311.   What is the landlocked Central European country bordering
        Germany, Italy, and the Czech Republic?
        Austria

312.   Name the landlocked Eastern European country bordering
        Lithuania, Latvia, and Poland.
        Belarus

313.   Name the three northwestern European states who are members
        of the Benelux Customs Union.
        Belgium, Netherlands, Luxembourg

314.   Kauhajoki is a city in the Southern Ostrobothnia region of what
        European country?
        Finland

315. The Wicklow Mountains are in what European country that has Cork as its southernmost and largest county?
Ireland

316. Name the city located on the eastern side of the Mersey Estuary that was named the European Capital of Culture.
Liverpool

317. The Barajas International Airport is located in what European capital city on the Manzanares River?
Madrid

318. What country borders Latvia, Belarus, and Poland?
Lithuania

319. Name the largest country entirely within Europe that has a coastline on the Black Sea and the Sea of Azov.
Ukraine

320. What European country borders the Kaliningrad oblast and Germany?
Poland

321. The "Colossus" of this island, the largest of the Dodecanese Islands in the Hellenic Republic, as well as its Old Town have made it a UNESCO World Heritage Site. Name this island.
Rhodes

322. Leopoldville, named after the younger son of King Leopold III, is located in the Democratic Republic of the Congo. Name the country of which King Leopold III was a ruler.
Belgium

323. What Mediterranean microstate east of Tunisia is the most densely populated in Europe?
Malta

324. Gothenburg, or Göteborg, is the second-largest city in which Nordic country that is linked to Denmark by the Oresund Bridge?
Sweden

325. What landlocked country is comprised of the historic regions of Moravia, Bohemia, and parts of Silesia and was formed after the peaceful Velvet Revolution?
Czech Republic

326. Northern Europe's oldest cathedral is the Aachen Cathedral. This is in which European country?
Germany

327. Painted churches in the Bucovina region, also known as Northern Moldavia, are a testament to the rich artistic culture of which European country?
Romania

328. Name Scandinavia's largest city, home to the Biological Museum and the Nordic Museum.
Stockholm

329. What Mediterranean country has Gozo and Comino as two of its three inhabited islands?
Malta

330. During World War II, the second-largest town in the Auvergne region of France served as the capital of the "non-occupied" region in the country during German occupation in World War II. Name this well-known spa town.
Vichy

331. Name the largest city entirely in Europe as of 2011.
Moscow

332. As of August 2010 European Union's leading agricultural exporter is also the world's second largest agricultural producer after United States. Name this country.
France

CHAPTER 5

Africa

1. In 1935, under Mussolini's orders, Italian general De Bono invaded Ethiopia. At that time, Ethiopia was known by what name?
Abyssinia

2. In 1895, French troops occupied the city of Antananarivo after the refusal of Prime Minister Rainilaiarivony to agree to French sovereignty. This city is in what Indian Ocean island country?
Madagascar

3. The Bijagos Islands belong to what West African country?
Guinea-Bissau

4. Which one of these choices does not belong and why: Tripoli, Benghazi, Ghadamis, and Derna.
Ghadamis, because it is not a port city on the Mediterranean Sea

5. Gondar, the center of an African empire in the 17th and 18th centuries, lies north of Lake Tana and southwest of the Simien Mountains in what present-day country?
Ethiopia

6. Lake Langano and Lake Shala are scenic areas in a country that borders Eritrea and Somalia. These lakes are in what well-known valley?
Great Rift Valley

7. Name the African country that has Limpopo as its northernmost province?
South Africa

8. The capital of North Kivu province, in eastern Democratic Republic of the Congo, continues to experience the effects of the Rwandan genocide to this day. Name this city.
Goma

9. Name the African nation bordering Uganda and Tanzania that has a lingering ethnic conflict, resulting from the traditionally unequal relationship between the dominant Tutsi minority and the Hutu majority.
   Rwanda

10. Since its independence in 1961, an African country on Lake Tanganyika continues to suffer from a conflict between its dominant Tutsi minority and the Hutu majority. Name this country.
    Burundi

11. Elephantine Island, the site of the Nubian Museum, lies on what body of water?
    Nile River

12. The Ptolemaic Temple in Edfu is one of the largest temples in what African country?
    Egypt

13. The cities of Agadir and Essaouira are in what Arab country that has a constitutional monarchy?
    Morocco

14. Fort Dauphin, also known as Tolarano, was once an important French settlement in what country that has the Mozambique Channel on its western coast?
    Madagascar

15. What country, whose name translates in local dialects to "homeland of the proud people," borders Ghana and Mali?
    Burkina Faso

16.   In 1976 during the Idi Amin dictatorship, Israeli commandos
        made a daring rescue of hostages in what Ugandan city on Lake
        Victoria near Kampala?
        Entebbe

17.   In October 1942, the Allies defeated the Axis forces at the Battle
        of El Alamein in what African country?
        Egypt

18.   In 1951, what African country became the first to gain
        independence through the United Nations?
        Libya (from Italy)

19.   Name the oldest independent country in Africa.
        Ethiopia

20.   What monument in Egypt is often regarded as the largest temple
        complex ever built?
        Temple of Karnak

21.   Name the provincial capital of Gauteng, the wealthiest province
        in South Africa.
        Johannesburg

22.   The Ogaden National Liberation Front has often carried out
        attacks against the government of what landlocked country on the
        Horn of Africa?
        Ethiopia

23.   Name the second-largest city in Egypt that is often known as the
        Pearl of the Mediterranean.
        Alexandria

24.   Name the world-famous falls in southern Africa that consist of
        Main Falls, Devils Cataract, and Rainbow Falls.
        Victoria Falls National Park

25. Douala, on the banks of the Wouri River, is the largest seaport in what country that borders the Republic of the Congo and Gabon?
Cameroon

26. Kananga, a city on the Kasai River, is in what central African country that is bordered by Angola to the south?
Democratic Republic of the Congo

27. The Hector Pieterson Monument, commemorating the end of apartheid, is in what South African city that has the township of Soweto within its confines?
Johannesburg

28. Kerma was the capital of what African kingdom situated in what was then the home of the Nubian people?
Kush

29. In 2006, Little Selam, the fossilized remains of a human infant that lived 100,000 years earlier than Lucy, was discovered in the northeastern part of what African country?
Ethiopia

30. The Movement for the Emancipation of the Niger Delta, a rebel group in a West African OPEC country that gained independence from the United Kingdom on October 1, 1960, has been a constant irritant for the government of what country?
Nigeria

31. Providing aid to the sensitive eastern Ogaden region has been a major challenge for international agencies in Somali state of what African country?
Ethiopia

32. Historic Kilwa Kisiwani and Songo Mnara Ruins are found in what country well known for its Ngorongoro Conservation Area?
Tanzania

33. Name the West African capital city, named for enslaved Africans who fought for the British in the American Revolutionary War that is situated near the world's third-largest natural harbor.
Freetown

34. Plans have been made to move a giant statue of Ramses II from Ramses Square in Cairo to a home near the great pyramids to halt the statue's degradation from pollution. This statue was originally situated in what ancient capital city of Egypt?
Memphis

35. Dahab, a world-famous tourist center for windsurfing, scuba diving, and snorkeling, is a small town on the southeast coast of what country in the Middle East?
Egypt

36. Honey is the main livelihood of the Shenko people who live on the edges of a highland forest in a country bordering Sudan, South Sudan, and Eritrea. Name this country.
Ethiopia

37. There are important gold mines at Elandsrand in an African country that owns the Prince Edward Islands, a sub-Antarctic archipelago. Name this country.
South Africa

38. Bo is the second-largest city of what African country bordered by Guinea and Liberia?
Sierra Leone

39. Bakassi, controlled by Cameroon, is the peninsular extension of Calabar, the capital of the Cross River state in what country?
Nigeria

40. The Mala Mala Game Reserve is in what African country that borders Namibia and Swaziland?
South Africa

41. Many European cave paintings have similarities to patterns found in the paintings of people from what South African tribe?
San

42. During the "Golden War," the Nubians of Kush, who were often known as the Black Pharaohs, battled what empire in Africa?
Egyptian Empire

43. An archaeological site in Cyrene, in an African country, has the largest necropolis in the world. Name this country.
Libya

44. Bhoutros Bhoutros Gali, the first Arab Secretary General of the United Nations, hailed from what country that has the well-known remote oasis city of Siwa, which lies less than 20 miles from this country's border with Libya?
Egypt

45. The Ubangi River and the Kasai River are tributaries of the largest river in western central Africa. Name this river.
Congo River

46. In 1879, about 8,000 people from an African tribe died defending their country from the British in southern Africa. The Natal province in South Africa was renamed to reflect the reality of the major presence of these Ngunu-speaking tribes in the post-apartheid era. Name this tribe.
Zulus

47. The Mzima Springs, favorite haunts for hippos and crocodiles, can be found in what African country bordering the Indian Ocean between Somalia and Tanzania?
     Kenya

48. Named after a river of the same name, the Luangwa National Park is in what African country that is home to a large population of hippos and crocodiles?
     Zambia

49. What is the largest city in East Africa?
     Nairobi

50. Lamu Island, once an Arab trading center and a famous spice center, is the oldest living town of what East African country?
     Kenya

51. According to reports, the quiver tree, a famed desert tree used by Africa's Bushmen to make quivers, is threatened by global warming. The quiver tree has iconic status in what African country that has Walvis Bay as its largest seaport?
     Namibia

52. The Afar people speak Cushitic, an ancient tongue from the highlands of what African country?
     Ethiopia

53. Name the only African country that is not a member of the African Union.
     Morocco

54. The Awash River is a river that never makes it to the sea. Instead, it sinks into a salt lake on the border of what two African countries?
     Ethiopia and Djibouti

55. If you are visiting Greek and Roman ruins in the Benghazi area, you are in what African country?
Libya

56. The Virunga National Park is located in the northeast of what African country that borders Zambia?
Democratic Republic of the Congo

57. The Amarna Period was a time of spectacular events in the history of what Middle Eastern country?
Egypt

58. In 1861, three years after reaching Lake Tanganyika, Sir Richard Burton became the first man to ascend the highest mountain in west Africa. This mountain is in what country near the Gulf of Guinea?
Cameroon

59. Majority of the Dinka tribes are found in the swamplands of the Bahr el Ghazal region of the Nile basin in the northwestern part of what country that borders the Democratic Republic of the Congo, Ethiopia, and Kenya?
South Sudan

60. Because of its concentration of rock art, the Tsodilo Hills, in the Kalahari Desert, have often been called the "Louvre of the desert." This UNESCO World Heritage Site lies in what country that borders Zimbabwe?
Botswana

61. The oases of Ghadames and Kufra are in what North African country that became a non-permanent UN Security Council member in October 2007?
Libya

62. A Mediterranean wind that comes from the Sahara reaches hurricane speed in Libya, where it is known as the qibli. Name this wind.
Sirocco

63. What African group lives along the famous Bandiagara Escarpment, a rocky outcropping near a city in the Sahara that was once a center of commerce but is now the end of the old salt trail?
Dogon People

64. In 1889 the Uhuru Peak on Kibo was named Kaiser-Wilhelm-Spitze, before changing back to its original name in 1918 when Germany was defeated in World War I. Uhuru Peak is the highest point of what mountain in Africa?
Mt. Kilimanjaro

65. Belgium once controlled mining interests in the province of Katanga in what African country?
Democratic Republic of the Congo

66. The Wadi Al-Hitan or Valley of the Whales, was an ancient seabed in Africa. It is now a stretch of sand dunes in the Western Desert of what Arab country?
Egypt

67. Mogador is the former name of what port city and tourist resort in western Morocco?
Essaouira

68. What country produces the most cocoa in the world?
Cote d'Ivoire

69. Name the largest city in the South African province of KwaZulu-Natal.
Durban

70. Name the landlocked country in West Africa bordered by Cote d'Ivoire to its southwest and formerly known as the Republic of Upper Volta.
Burkina Faso

71. Puntland is an autonomous region in the northeast of what country located on the Horn of Africa?
Somalia

72. Name the west African country west of Benin that has its capital on the coast of the Gulf of Guinea.
Togo

73. Mount Tahat, Algeria's highest peak, is located in what mountain range?
Ahaggar Mountains

74. The African Union, a pan-African union to promote peace and prosperity on the continent, is headquartered in what capital city?
Addis Ababa

75. The Ebola virus, named after a river of the same name, was first identified in an African country that is bordered by South Sudan to the northeast and Angola to the southwest. Name this country.
Democratic Republic of Congo

76. Sometimes called the eighth wonder of the world, the Ngorongoro Crater hosts more than 20,000 animals in the dry season. This crater is in what African country?
Tanzania

77. The Masai Mara in Kenya is the northern portion of what famous park where animals cross Tanzania and Kenya in search of the best grazing grounds?
Serengeti National Park

78.   The world's highest sand dunes are found in what African country?
      Namibia

79.   South Africa's Free State borders what country?
      Lesotho

80.   Lake Kariba, often called the largest man-made lake in the world,
      lies on the border between what two African countries?
      Zambia and Zimbabwe

81.   The 2010 World Cup Soccer was held in what country in the
      Southern Hemisphere that has the famous tourist sites of False
      Bay, Cape Point, and the Cape of Good Hope?
      South Africa

82.   Port Harcourt is the capital of what Nigerian state near the Niger
      River Delta?
      Rivers State

83.   If you are tasting a Malagasy dish of rice and seafood cooked with
      coconut milk at Nosy Be, a tiny coastal island, you are in what
      African country?
      Madagascar

84.   Al-Maghreb-Al Aqsa is the Arabic name for what country that has
      Agadir as one of its important cities?
      Morocco

85.   The Temple of Horus is one of the best preserved masterpieces of
      the ancient world. This temple is in an African country that lies
      directly north of Sudan. Name this country.
      Egypt

86.   Lake Nakuru National Park, a major retreat for flamingoes, is in
      the Great Rift Valley of what East African country?
      Kenya

87. In 1897, Governor Martini from Italy made what city the colonial capital instead of that colony's popular Red Sea port city of Massawa?
Asmara

88. Thabo Mbeki, a member of the African National Congress, is the president of what country that has the famous Kruger National Park?
South Africa

89. The famous Muslim traveler Ibn Batuta was born in Tangier, a city on the north African coast at the western entrance to the Strait of Gibraltar where the Mediterranean meets the Atlantic Ocean. Tangier is located in what country?
Morocco

90. The 23rd-century B.C.E. Egyptian nobleman Harkhuf was one of the pioneer explorers of his time. His tomb can be found in the city of Elephantine, which is now part of which modern city?
Aswan

91. In 1415, the capital city of Ceuta gave Portugal access to what present-day country on the African mainland?
Morocco

92. A lake in Malawi is named after the Swahili word for lake. Name this lake.
Nyasa

93. Lakoja, at the confluence of the Niger and Benue rivers, was a major trading settlement in 1864. Lakoja is in what present-day country?
Nigeria

94. What ancient culture is known to worship Ra, the sun god?
Egyptian

95. The equator and the prime meridian cross in what body of water off the coast of Africa?
Gulf of Guinea

96. In August 2005, emergency centers were erected by Doctors without Borders in the town of Maradi to combat hunger in what western African country that gained independence from France in 1960?
Niger

97. Francistown is the second-largest city in what African country?
Botswana

98. The village of Umoja, which means unity in Swahili, is adjacent to Samburu National Reserve in what African country?
Kenya

99. In 1424 C.E., Portuguese explorer Prince Henry the Navigator sent his people to explore "Bulging Cape", south of the Canaries in West Africa. This cape is known by what modern name?
Cape Bojador or Cape Boujdour

100. Name the country that does not belong and explain why: Burundi, Democratic Republic of Congo, Rwanda, Tanzania, Zambia.
Rwanda, because it does not border Lake Tanganyika

101. Arusha National Park, overlooking Mount Meru, is in what African country bordering Rwanda?
Tanzania

102. The Goualougo Triangle, a 100-square-mile region that is home to the world's highest density of chimpanzees in Equatorial Africa, is located in the Sangha region of what country that is bounded by Gabon to its west?
Republic of Congo

103. Following the defeat at Waterloo, Napoleon was exiled to a 47-square-mile island named St. Helena in the Atlantic Ocean. This island is about 1,200 miles due west of what African country?
Angola

104. Ile Coco Marine National Park is in what island nation situated about 1,000 miles east of Kenya?
Seychelles

105. The ruins of Leptis Magna and Sabrata are reminders of the Roman invasion of what Arab country?
Libya

106. The Acacus Mountains represent one of the areas of wildest nature inhabited in the Sahara. These mountains lie southwest of the Fezzan area of what African country?
Libya

107. The ancient town of Djenne, famous for its Great Mosque, one of the world's largest mud brick structures, is in what country?
Mali

108. In 1482, Portuguese explorer Diego Cao landed at Cape Santa Maria in what present-day African country?
Angola

109. Rare desert elephants are sometimes found in the heart of Kaokoland in what African country that borders Angola and Zambia?
Namibia

110. In 1925, Belgians established a well-known national park for mountain gorillas in the Democratic Republic of the Congo. Name this park.
Virunga National Park

111. In 2006, the court of what country ruled that Bushmen can hunt and live in their ancestral lands near the Central Kalahari Game Reserve?
Botswana

112. The Bodele Depression, flanked by enormous basalt mountain ranges, is a dry lake bed in Africa. This lake bed was once part of what lake?
Lake Chad

113. In 2007, what small country that has the loti as its currency became the largest exporter of clothing to the United States from sub-Saharan Africa?
Lesotho

114. On February 5, 2007, Asha-Rose Migiro became the second woman in history to take office as the UN Deputy Secretary General. She hails from an African country that borders Uganda and Malawi. Name this country.
Tanzania

115. Tamashek, an Afro-Asiatic language whose script is related to ancient Libyan, is spoken by a group of African people, in which men wear characteristic blue-colored robes and bound headdresses. What is the name of this group?
Tuaregs

116. The Etosha Pans are located in what African country?
Namibia

117. Fderik is an important iron-ore mining village in what country that borders Algeria?
Mauritania

118. Name the Angolan province that has a border with the Republic of the Congo and the Democratic Republic of the Congo.
Cabinda

119. In February 2007, a rebellion started in part of the Sahara desert that is home to some of the world's largest uranium deposits. What is the name of the Berber ethnic group that is demanding a greater share in this mineral wealth?
Tuaregs

120. What is the name of the hydroelectric dam whose construction resulted in the creation of Lake Volta, the world's largest man-made lake?
Akosombo Dam

121. Name the port city in Namibia that was under South African rule until 1994.
Walvis Bay

122. What is the name of the gulf that partially bifurcates Djibouti into two parts?
Gulf of Tadjoura

123. Northern Africa became part of the Roman Empire after what wars?
Punic Wars

124. What African country has the famous Djenne Mosque?
Mali

125. Wole Soyinka was the first African to win the Nobel Prize in Literature. He was born in 1934 at Abeokuta, near Ibadan, the capital of Oyo state, in what West African country?
Nigeria

126. Wangari Maathai's fight to stop deforestation in Africa gained her so much acclaim that she became the first African woman to win the Nobel Peace Prize in 2004. Maathai hails from what East African country?
Kenya

127.   Put in order, from east to west: Burkina Faso, Tunisia, Chad
        Chad, Tunisia, Burkina Faso

128.   Manda National Park and the museum and handicraft centre of
        Sarh are tourist attractions in the middle-Chari region of which
        landlocked African country?
        Chad

129.   Nearly 1,500 years ago, a major African tribe drove the Baswara
        tribe (also known as the San) to near extinction as they pushed
        them south from central Africa. These tribes now live primarily in
        the regions that straddle the equator and continue southward into
        southern Africa. Name this tribe.
        Bantu

130.   Name Kenya's largest province by area.
        Rift Valley

131.   Bandar Beyla and Bosasa are administrative regions in the Bari
        region of what country on the Horn of Africa?
        Somalia

132.   The Great Temple of Amun, one of Egypt's most sacred sites, is in
        what temple complex near Luxor?
        Karnak

133.   What member of the WTO that gained independence from
        Portugal in 1975 is located in the mid-Atlantic Ocean about 300
        mi. off the west coast of Africa?
        Cape Verde

134.   Name the landlocked country that was once part of French
        Equatorial Africa and known as Ubangi-Shari.
        Central African Republic

135. Adamawa, Delta, and Plateau are states in what West African oil-rich country?
Nigeria

136. The city of Biltine is located in the Wadi Fira region of what country bordered by Nigeria and Cameroon to its southwest?
Chad

137. The Benadir region spans Africa's coast from the Gulf of Aden to the Juba River. This region is in what African country?
Somalia

138. Marsa Matrouh is a seaport about 150 miles west of Alexandria and is located in what country, the most populous in North Africa?
Egypt

139. What landlocked southern African country that has English as its official language has been known for its high rate of inflation?
Zimbabwe

140. Oil production is a major industry on Bonny Island, which is located at the southern edge of Rivers State in the Niger Delta of what country?
Nigeria

141. Name the country separated from Senegal by the Senegal River and whose capital is Nouakchott.
Mauritania

142. South Africa's third most populous city, located on the Indian Ocean, claims to be the busiest port in Africa. Name this city.
Durban

143. Name the oil-rich lake located in the center of Africa on the
border of Uganda and the Democratic Republic of the Congo and
to the northeast of Lake Edward.
Lake Albert

144. Name the second-largest city in the Maghreb after Casablanca,
home to the Casbah.
Algiers

145. The city of Mongu, just east of the Zambezi River, overlooks the
Barotse Plains in an African country that has a shoreline along
Lake Tanganyika. Name this country.
Zambia

146. What country owns the Dahlak Archipelago?
Eritrea

147. Name the landlocked country that shares Lake Mweru with the
Democratic Republic of the Congo?
Zambia

148. Name the southern African country that shares Victoria Falls with
Zambia and whose major language is Shona.
Zimbabwe

149. Name the country on the Horn of Africa whose capital is on the
Wabe Shabeelle?
Somalia

150. The province of Mpumalanga, formerly known as Eastern
Transvaal, is located in what African country?
South Africa

151. The largest country on the Mediterranean Sea is also the largest country in Africa. Name this country.
Algeria

152. Name the African country, once colonized by Italy, which has the only national flag in the world with just one color—green.
Libya

153. What African country, bordering Burkina Faso to the north and Ghana to the west, has its capital on the Gulf of Guinea?
Togo

154. Kgalema Motlanthe was the third post-apartheid president of what African country?
South Africa

155. What mainland country has the longest coastline in Africa?
Somalia

156. Jos, the administrative capital of the Plateau State, is in what African country bordering Cameroon?
Nigeria

157. Name the West African country, west of Togo, where Ashanti Twi is spoken by majority of the population?
Ghana

158. The city of Brazzaville is closest to what other capital city?
Kinshasa

159. Name the gulf off the Horn of Africa.
Gulf of Aden

160.   The sources of the Niger, the Gambia, and the Senegal rivers are
        in what West African nation?
        Guinea

161.   Name the small landlocked country east of Lake Kivu.
        Rwanda

162.   Kufra Airport is located in what country that has Tripolitania, the
        Fezzan, and Cyrenaica as its three main regions?
        Libya

163.   Albert Schweitzer's hospital is a major attraction in the city of
        Lambarene in what country west of the Republic of Congo?
        Gabon

164.   The Osun-Osogbo Sacred Grove in Osogbo (Oshogbo) is a sacred
        forest that is the cradle of the cultural traditions of a West African
        ethnic group in what country?
        Nigeria

165.   Name the seaport in north-west Madagascar located on the red,
        silt saturated delta of the Betsiboka River.
        Mahajanga

CHAPTER 6

Asia

1. The island of Ceram, part of the Moluccas archipelago, belongs to what country?
Indonesia

2. If you are in the geisha area of Gion, you are in what Asian country bordered by the Pacific Ocean to the east?
Japan

3. The Wakhan Corridor belongs to what Asian country?
Afghanistan

4. Kampong Ayer, often called the largest water village in the world, is in what Asian capital city that was visited by Magellan in 1521?
Bandar Seri Begawan, Brunei

5. Ama Dablam, which means "mother of pearl necklace," is a 22,349-foot mountain in the Himalayan range where mountaineers train before embarking on an Everest expedition. Ama Dablam is in what country?
Nepal

6. What is the name of the river that links the Mekong River to the largest lake in Cambodia that shares the same name?
Tonle Sap River

7. Male is a major town in what Indian Ocean country that has Dhivehi as its official language?
Maldives

8. To visit the pre-Angkorian ruins of Wat Phou, you will visit what landlocked Asian country that borders China?
Laos

9.   The Pashupatinath Temple, a sacred temple of Shiva, is in what Hindu-majority country known for its famous Dudh Kosi River in the Khumbu Valley?
     Nepal

10. Name the country that has Mount Kinabalu as its highest peak.
     Malaysia

11. Mount Chomolhari, otherwise known as the Mountain of the Goddess, is the source of the Paro Chu River, which nourishes the Paro Valley. This 23,996-foot peak is the second-highest peak in what Asian country?
     Bhutan

12. Name the legendary marble monument, built by the Moghul emperor Shah Jahan in 1648 C.E., in the city of Agra in India.
     Taj Mahal

13. The "Long March" marked the turning point in the history of what Asian country?
     China

14. In March 1946, with the help of the USSR, a group in Iran formed the Mahabad Republic with its capital Mahabad in northwestern Iran. This republic was later disbanded as Iran reasserted control of the region in June 1946. Name this group.
     Kurds

15. During World War I, T. E. Lawrence, a British soldier, adventurer, and military strategist who became famous as Lawrence of Arabia, helped lead an Arab revolt against what empire?
     Ottoman Empire

16. What treaty in 1920 formally ended the Ottoman Empire?
     The Treaty of Sévres

17. Golda Meir the first female prime minister, served what Middle
     Eastern country between 1969 and 1974?
     Israel

18. Ranthambore National Park, once the private hunting grounds of
     the Maharajas, and home of the famous Bengal Tiger, is in what
     Asian country?
     India

19. Jomsom is the gateway to Tibetan biomes and the vast desert
     valley of Mustang. Jomsom is in what Himalayan country?
     Nepal

20. What is the name of the most populous city of the Philippines,
     which functioned as its capital from 1948 to 1976?
     Quezon City

21. What is the name of the city that lies at the confluence of the
     Gombak and Klang rivers?
     Kuala Lumpur

22. The Jeju Volcanic Island and Lava Tube, a UNESCO World
     Heritage Site that includes Geomunoreum, one of the finest lava
     tube systems of caves, is in what Asian country?
     South Korea

23. Lake Toba, a vast volcanic caldera with the Asahan River as its primary
     outflow, is the largest volcanic lake in the world. The site of an ancient
     Stone Age super eruption, this lake is in what Asian country?
     Indonesia

24. In 2007, eleven new species were discovered in the "Green Corridor,"
     a remote region near the Annamites mountain range in the
     easternmost nation on the Indochina peninsula. Name this country.
     Vietnam

25. Name Bangladesh's chief seaport and its second largest city.
Chittagong

26. Changi Airport is a major airport in what small Asian island country north of the Riau Archipelago in Indonesia?
Singapore

27. The city of Leh, capital of the Ladakh region on the Indus River, is in what Asian country that borders China?
India

28. Name the high-tech capital city of the Indian state of Karnataka that is located on the Precambrian Deccan Plateau.
Bangalore

29. Tiger Leaping Gorge, one of the deepest gorges in the world, is in the Yunnan province of what Asian country?
China

30. The capital city of Kazakhstan, Astana, lies on the banks of what river?
Ishim

31. What is the capital of the Iraqi province of Anbar?
Ramadi

32. In the 480 B.C.E. Battle of Salamis, Greek forces successfully thwarted the invasion of what major Asian empire?
Persian Empire

33. The island of Olkhon, one of the biggest islands of Russia, lies on what body of water?
Lake Baikal

34. What is the name of the only major Japanese island that does not border the Inland Sea?
Hokkaido

35. The 1914 WWI Battle of the Vistula River, also known as the Battle of Warsaw, was fought between Germany and what other country?
Russia

36. What present-day city was the first capital of British India in 1772?
Kolkata

37. The Minaret of Jam, a site that is in the list of endangered UNESCO World Heritage Sites, is in the Ghor province of what Asian country that borders Uzbekistan and Iran?
Afghanistan

38. India's southernmost point, on Great Nicobar, is just north of the largest island belonging entirely to Indonesia. Name this island.
Sumatra

39. The westernmost point of India lies in what Indian state?
Gujarat

40. One of the seven emirates of the UAE has land in both the Persian Gulf and the Arabian Sea. Name this emirate that borders Dubai.
Sharjah

41. What is the name of the island located on the eastern side of the Persian Gulf, near the entrance of the Strait of Hormuz that is claimed by both Iran and the UAE?
Abu Musa

42. The US Bagram Air Force base is located next to the ancient city of Bagram in what south Asian country?
Afghanistan

43. Lorentz National Park, one of the world's most ecologically
     diverse national parks containing ecosystems that range from
     snow caps to a tropical marine environment, lies in what
     Southeast Asian country?
     Indonesia

44. What body of water borders the Malaysian state of Perak to its
     west?
     Strait of Malacca

45. Muslims living in southern Mindanao and the Sulu Archipelago
     of the Philippines are commonly known by what name?
     Moros

46. The Penang Bridge, one of the world's longest bridges, is in what
     Asian country?
     Malaysia

47. What is the name of the southernmost province of Malaysia that
     lies just north of Singapore?
     Johor

48. The Crocker Range forms the backbone of what Malaysian state
     on the island of Borneo?
     Sabah

49. In 1826, the British added what Asian country to Malacca and
     Penang, on the Malay Peninsula, to form the British Malaya?
     Singapore

50. What is the name of the Chinese province on the country's
     southern coast bordering Hong Kong?
     Guangdong

51. Victoria Harbor separates the Kowloon Peninsula from what Chinese island?
     Hong Kong

52. What major Russian freshwater river flows into the northern Caspian Sea making it less salty than its southern part?
     Volga

53. Dharamsala, the town that became a home for the Dalai Lama and the exiled Tibetan community, is in what country?
     India

54. Alfred Nobel used revenues from his oil fields to fund a portion of the money given to Nobel Prize winners. Name the largest city in Azerbaijan, where these oil fields are located.
     Baku

55. Name the disputed Armenian-dominated enclave within the borders of Azerbaijan.
     Nagorno-Karabakh

56. Ashura is a remembrance day for a famous 680 C.E. battle between the Shiites and the Sunnis. This battle took place on the hot and dusty plain of what city in present-day Iraq?
     Karbala

57. What is the name of the Malaysian city that was captured by the Dutch from the Portuguese in 1641 and held till almost 1824?
     Malacca

58. The 1998 Winter Olympics were held in Nagano in what Asian country?
     Japan

59. In 2007, French archaeologists excavated an 11,000-year old wall painting, the world's oldest wall painting, at the Neolithic settlement of Djade al-Mughara on the Euphrates, northeast of the city of Aleppo. This site is in what country?
Syria

60. The 338-square-mile island of Majuli, one of the largest river islands in the world, lies nearly 220 miles east of Assam state's largest city, Gauhati, in India. Majuli is on what river?
Brahmaputra River

61. Papua is the largest province by area of what Asian country?
Indonesia

62. The Sunni-dominated Anbar Province, with Ramadi as its capital city, is the largest province in what Middle Eastern country?
Iraq

63. What strait in Asia is popularly known as the Taiwan Strait?
Formosa Strait

64. Name the mountains that separate the Deccan Plateau from the Indo-Gangetic Plain.
Vindhya Mountains

65. Nalchik is the capital of the mostly Muslim republic of Kabardino-Balkariya in what country in the Eastern Hemisphere?
Russia

66. Which island has Russia's easternmost point?
Big Diomede Island

67. Name the banana-like plant that is also known as Manila hemp.
Abaca

68. Ferdinand Magellan was killed by the Chief Lapu-Lapu on what Philippine island near Cebu?

Mactan

69. The largest city in the Philippines in terms of land area is on Mindanao. Name this city.

Davao

70. According to scientists, a major earthquake occurred about 75,000 years ago near Lake Toba, on an island in Indonesia. Name this island.

Sumatra

71. The Western Ghats and the Eastern Ghats merge in the southern state of Tamil Nadu in what Asian country?

India

72. The Akashi Kaikyo Bridge connects which two major Japanese islands?

Shikoku and Honshu

73. Name the region in Turkey that is home to a unique field of cones and underground cities where Christians once hid to avoid persecution from Roman soldiers.

Cappadocia

74. Name the item that does not belong and explain why: Narmada River, Ganges River, Godavari River, Brahmaputra River.

Narmada River, because it does not empty into the Bay of Bengal

75. The city of Allahabad, located at the confluence of the Ganges and the Yamuna rivers, is one of the four sites of the Kumbha Mela, one of the largest Hindu gatherings in the world. This city is in what state in north India?

Uttar Pradesh

76. What historical city was formerly known as Angora?
Ankara

77. During the 1942 Doolittle Raid, Americans bombed the mainland of what Asian country?
Japan

78. The Mooncake Festival or Mid-Autumn Festival, celebrated by moon gazing and eating moon cakes, falls on the 15th day of the eighth month of what Asian calendar system?
Chinese calendar

79. Adam's Peak has been the object of worship and pilgrimage for over 1,000 years. This is one of the highest peaks in what country where Sinhalese is spoken by the majority of the people?
Sri Lanka

80. Japan's Kansai International Airport is on an artificial island in what body of water?
Osaka Bay

81. Japan's Narita International Airport, in Tokyo, is in what prefecture?
Chiba

82. The English words *khaki*, *paradise*, and *pajamas* came from a language that originated in a country bordering Afghanistan. Name this language.
Farsi

83. The well-known poet Omar Khayyam, who wrote the *Rubaiyat*, hailed from what Asian country?
Iran

84. The Khmer Water Festival is a regular feature in what Asian country?
Cambodia

85. Rudyard Kipling was born in India's most populous city. Name this city.
Mumbai

86. Zard Kuh is the highest point in what mountains in Iran?
Zagros Mountains

87. Name the East Asian country, one of world's largest shipbuilders, that lies to the east of the Yellow Sea.
South Korea

88. Mindoro Island is in what Asian country?
Philippines

89. Dagestan is a federal subject of what large transcontinental country?
Russia

90. Name the largest country in the Arab Middle East.
Saudi Arabia

91. The statue of a griffin is one of the major attractions of an ancient Iranian city that served as the capital of the ancient Persian Empire in the 5ᵗʰ to 6ᵗʰ century B.C.E.. Name this city.
Persepolis

92. A great mound of man-made debris about sixty feet high and almost a mile across is the highlight of an ancient city about a hundred miles south of Baghdad. Name this holy city.
Nippur

93. What oil-rich Shiite country borders the Persian Gulf, the Gulf of Oman, and the Caspian Sea?
Iran

94. The medieval city of Kufah and what other Iraqi holy city are drained by both the Tigris and the Euphrates rivers?
Karbala

95. The 1953 truce that halted the Korean War was signed in a village that straddles the border between North Korea and South Korea. Name this village.
Panmunjom

96. Which country owns the largest islands in the Hanish Island group in the Red Sea?
Yemen

97. The Taal Volcano, south of the Philippines' capital Manila, is situated on what island?
Luzon

98. The lost city of Tortosa, as the Crusaders called it, is now the city of Tartus. Tartus is the largest city in the Tartus Governate of what present-day country in Southwest Asia that borders the Mediterranean Sea?
Syria

99. The Nabateans, an ancient trading people of southern Jordan, carved a city into mountains in the Middle East and then abandoned it 2,000 years ago. What is the name of this city that has now become a must-see monument in that country?
Petra

100. Name Russia's largest island.
Sakhalin

101. The Yali tribe is found in the western part of what large island in Southeast Asia that is separated from Australia by the Torres Strait?
New Guinea

102. What Chinese province, known for the historic city of Dali, is drained by the Yangtze, the Salween, and the Mekong Rivers?
Yunnan

103. Minicoy Island, also known as Maliku, belongs to what Asian country?
India

104. Orangutans are conserved in the Mawas Forest Reserve in what Indonesian province in Borneo?
Kalimantan

105. What is the name of the country that stretches from Taiwan in the north to the island of Sulawesi in the south and was known to travelers as the Pearl of the Orient?
Philippines

106. Manila Bay, one of the best natural harbors of the world, serves what Philippine island?
Luzon

107. Al-Quds is the Arabic name for what holy city in the Middle East?
Jerusalem

108. Jafar-al-Mansour, who died in 775 C.E., was the founder of what present-day Middle Eastern capital city?
Baghdad

109. Mt. Kinabalu, known for its great botanical and biological diversity, lies in what Malaysian province that lies just west of the Sulu Sea?
Sabah

110. What popular holiday center that is often called Bird Island is located near the ancient city of Ephesus, facing the Greek island of Samos, in the Aegean region of Turkey?
Kusadasi

111. The provincial capital city of Mataram, famous for its Mayura Water Palace, lies on what Indonesian island with the same name as the strait that separates this island from Bali to its west?
Lombok

112. What current Asian capital city, whose name means "red hero," was founded in 1600 as the home of the Living Buddha and later became a trading center on the caravan route between Russia and China?
Ulaan Bator

113. The indigenous Kombai people are tree people found in what Asian country that has territories on the world's largest equatorial island?
Indonesia

114. In 1503 Italian adventurer Ludovico de Varthema sailed to what Romans called Arabia Felix. What is the present-day name of this country?
Yemen

115. The Taif Accords, made in 1989, transferred power away from the president, traditionally given to Maronites, and invested it in a cabinet divided equally between Muslims and Christians, thereby ending the civil war in what Middle East country?
Lebanon

116. Name the largest river in Transcaucasia, a region that consists of the countries of Georgia, Armenia, and Azerbaijan.
Kura River

117. Laodicea was the chief city of the historic Lycus River Valley. What is the present-day name of the country where this valley is located?
Turkey

118. Egyptians and the Hittites fought a decisive battle in the city of Kadesh on the Orontes River in what present-day country?
Syria

119. Name the Asian country that stretches from the Sea of Okhotsk in the north to the East China Sea in the south.
Japan

120. In 2007, a tornado killed several people in the Anhui Province of what large Asian country?
China

121. Name the smallest Arab state that is linked to Saudi Arabia by the King Fahd Causeway.
Bahrain

122. Charkha, one of the earliest recorded spinning wheels, was used to weave cotton in what large, peninsular country that borders Myanmar and China?
India

123. The Battle of Marathon in 490 B.C.E. is famous because the Greeks halted the expansion of what great power?
Persia

124. Lashkar Gah is the capital of what province in Afghanistan that is named after a major river in the country?
Helmand

125. To attend the Tsechu, a religious festival where masked dancers depict the events from the life of Padmasambhava, the eighth-century Buddhist teacher, you would go to the historic Paro Valley in what country?
Bhutan

126. The archaeological dig at Catal Huyuk, a city that existed around 5,000 B.C.E., is in what country that witnessed a major World War I battle in its historic town of Gallipoli?
Turkey

127. The Bird's Nest National Stadium that can seat 100,000 spectators hosted the 2010 Summer Olympics in which Asian city about 50 miles from Badaling, a section of the Great Wall of China?
Beijing

128. Konya, a well-known weaving center of oriental rugs and carpets, is in what country on the Black Sea?
Turkey

129. Mosul and what other northern city in Iraq are ethnically rich areas with large numbers of Sunni Arabs, Kurds, and Turkmens?
Tal Afar

130. What country has 11 time zones and 143 million people?
Russia

131. What country, in the past, has often faced separatist movements in the regions of South Ossetia, Abkhazia, and Ajaria?
Georgia

132. Name the body of water west of the Makassar Strait and south of Kalimantan.
Java Sea

133. What Middle Eastern country has the provinces of Muthanna and
      Dhi Qar?
      Iraq

134. Agartala is the capital of the northeastern state of Tripura in what
      country that borders China and Bhutan?
      India

135. The mouths of the Irrawaddy and Salween rivers are in what
      country that borders India?
      Myanmar

136. The region of Akrotiri is located on what island in the Middle East
      south of Turkey that joined the European Union on May 1, 2004?
      Cyprus

137. The cities of Mashhad and Tabriz are located in what Asian
      country that borders Azerbaijan?
      Iran

138. The base at Akrotiri, Cyprus, is a sovereign area that belongs to
      what European country?
      United Kingdom

139. Uvs Nuur is a major lake located in an Asian country. Name this
      country.
      Mongolia

140. Name the city that does not belong and explain why: Bandung,
      Denpasar, Yogyakarta, Surabaya, Cirebon.
      Denpasar, because it is not on Java; it is on Bali

141. What Eurasian country has differences with the Kurdistan
      Workers Party, popularly known as the PKK, and has labeled it a
      terrorist group?
      Turkey

142. Name the isthmus that links Africa and Southwest Asia via the Sinai Peninsula.
Isthmus of Suez

143. The city of Aleppo, one of the oldest inhabited cities in history, is in the northwestern part of what Middle Eastern country?
Syria

144. Lake Balkhash is in the eastern part of what country bordering Uzbekistan?
Kazakhstan

145. Name the largest country, by area, in mainland Southeast Asia.
Thailand
(**Note:** Although the region of Asia situated east of the Indian subcontinent and south of China is considered Southeast Asia by some, and Myanmar would be the answer, some National Geographic sources treat Myanmar as part of South Asia and not Southeast Asia)

146. The historic town of Ghazni is situated in what mountainous Asian country that borders Pakistan and Uzbekistan?
Afghanistan

147. The Makassar Strait separates what two Asian islands?
Borneo and Sulawesi

148. The city of Perim lies closest to Africa across the Bab-el-Mandeb. Perim is in what country on the Arabian Peninsula?
Yemen

149. The large earth fill dam at Nurek, which supplies electricity to Dushanbe, is located on what river?
Vakhsh

150.   Pobeda Peak, at 24,406 feet, is the highest peak in what central
        Asian country?
        Kyrgyzstan

151.   The Chin and Naga Hills run along Myanmar's border with what
        Asian country?
        India

152.   In the 1905 Battle of Tsushima, the Japanese victory over what
        country brought an end to European imperialism in Asia?
        Russia

153.   What sea lies to the north of the island of Timor?
        Banda Sea

154.   In 333 B.C.E., Alexander the Great fought Darius III in the
        Battle of Issus near the narrow valley of the Taurus Mountains.
        Issus is in what present-day country?
        Turkey

155.   In the 1980s, the Battle of Abadan was fought on an island
        bounded on the west by the Shatt-al-Arab in the Khuzestan
        Province of what country?
        Iran

156.   A large asteroid struck a Russian region in east Siberia on June
        30th, 1908. This event is named after a river in Krasnoyarsk Krai,
        Russia's federal subject and second largest region. Name this
        event.
        Tunguska event

157.   The Chiang Kai-shek Memorial Park and a new 1,667-foot
        building are major attractions in what Asian capital city?
        Taipei (Taipei 101 is one of the tallest buildings in the world)

158. The Six-Day War of 1967 was fought between Israel and what Arab country besides Syria and Jordan?
Egypt

159. Lord Mahavira is the founder of what religion that originated in India?
Jainism

160. On December 15, 1945, Supreme Commander of Allied Forces, Gen. Douglas MacArthur, issued what directive that altered the shape of Japan's indigenous religious tradition?
Shinto Directive

161. Matteo Ricci, an Italian missionary, mastered the classical script of which Asian country and was known to have compiled its first European dictionary from 1583-1588 with his compatriot Michele Ruggieri?
China

162. Name the second largest of the former Soviet republics after Russia.
Kazakhstan

163. "Mandarin" comes from the word *mantri*, a term from what ancient India language?
Sanskrit

164. Yong Le, the third emperor of the Ming dynasty, founded the Forbidden City when he moved his capital from what city to Beijing?
Nanjing

165. Nanga Parbat, one of the tallest mountains in the world, is situated in the western Himalayas and lies to the south of a major river in that region. Name this river.
Indus River

166. Kong Fu Zi, a philosopher born around 551 B.C.E. in China, was known by what popular name?
Confucius

167. What form of healing, drawn on ancient Chinese principles, and now at the center of Daoist teachings, became very popular around the world?
Acupuncture

168. The Daoist center of Keelung is on what Asian island?
Taiwan

169. The Eighty-eight Temples are a popular Buddhist pilgrimage center on which Japanese island?
Shikoku

170. Religious manuscripts discovered at the ancient Middle East Essence monastery of Qumran are housed in a museum known as the "Shrine of the Book." Qumran overlooks what body of water?
Dead Sea

171. A Russian city that has Domodedovo as its international airport was in medieval times known as the "Wooden City." Name this city.
Moscow

172. The Sakha Republic, one of the world's largest sub-national bodies, is situated in which country?
Russia

173. In the 14th century, during the invasion of the Islamic state of Demak, the Hindu Javanese aristocracy fled to what Indonesian island?
Bali

174. Which Indonesian islands were once known as the "Gold Island" and the "Rice Island" in Sanskrit?
Sumatra and Java

175. These islands in Indonesia, first called the Spice Islands, were discovered by the Portuguese in 1509.
Moluccas

176. Balikpapan, the center of Indonesia's oil industry, is in what Indonesian province?
Kalimantan

177. Buddhists celebrate Waisak, an annual festival at the ninth-century Buddhist Mahayana monument in central Java, Indonesia. This UNESCO World Heritage center is known by what name?
Borobudur

178. Name the world's largest producer of rice.
China

179. The Bromo Mountain, one of the most popular tourist attractions in Indonesia, is actually a crater on the large Tengger Massif in the eastern part of what island?
Java

180. The longest river in Europe is in Russia. Name this river.
Volga River

181. Put the following three rivers in order, from longest to shortest: Irtysh, Lena, Yenisey.
Lena, Irtysh, Yenisey

182. The rock formation known as the Three Brothers is on the shores of the world's deepest lake. Name this lake.
Lake Baikal

183. Which Russian city lies at the confluence of the Volga and Oka rivers?
Nizhniy Novgorod

184. What country is the world's largest producer of natural gas?
Russia

185. The Peter and Paul Fortress is on an island at the mouth of the Neva River in what city?
St. Petersburg

186. What mineral resource is found in abundance in the Tunguska-Lena basin in Russia?
Coal

187. In 1854, Britain, allied with Turkey and France, went to war with what country over concerns about Turkey's control of the straits that gave access to the Mediterranean from the Black Sea.
Russia (Crimean War)

188. What Asian capital city lies on the Ciliwung River?
Jakarta

189. During the Ice Age, sea levels were low enough for mainland Southeast Asia to connect to the Indonesian islands lying on what continental shelf?
Sunda Shelf

190. Which Russian peninsula lies closest to United States?
Chukchi Peninsula

191. Name one of the two Russian republics that border the Caspian.
Dagestan or Kalmykia

192.   The Russian republics of Gorno Altay, Tuva, and Buryatia border
       what Asian country?
       Mongolia

193.   The world's only freshwater seal is found in what Russian body of water?
       Lake Baikal

194.   The town of Magadan, gateway to the Kolyma region in Russia,
       lies on what body of water?
       Sea of Okhotsk

195.   The Republic of Ingushetiya borders what former Soviet republic?
       Georgia

196.   What is the alphabet of the Russian language called?
       Cyrillic

197.   The Avars and the Darghis are Islamic communities found mainly
       in what Russian republic?
       Dagestan

198.   St. Nicholas' Chapel is in what city that is at the geographical
       center of Russia?
       Novosibirsk

199.   Because of large deposits of iron, what Russian region, known for
       a magnetic anomaly, reads compass needles incorrectly?
       Kursk (Kursk Magnetic Anomaly)

200.   What river originates in northern Russia's Valdai Hills in the
       Kalinin region?
       Volga River

201.   Name the large lake that lies closest to St. Petersburg.
       Lake Ladoga

202.   Name the only river flowing out of Lake Baikal.
        Angara River

203.   What was the 13th-century capital of the powerful Mongol state of
        "Rus" before Kublai Khan moved the Imperial capital to Beijing?
        Karakorum

204.   Modern Communism is based on Karl Marx's famous document
        about the communist ideology. His work is popularly known by
        what name?
        Das Kapital

205.   A barbed wire fence and observation towers built to segregate
        Eastern Europe from its western counterpart during the Cold War
        was referred to as what by historians?
        Iron Curtain

206.   Former countries of the USSR now remain a loose entity under
        the banner of the CIS. What does CIS stand for?
        Commonwealth of Independent States

207.   The Lower House of the Russian Parliament is known by what
        name?
        The Duma

208.   A centrally planned economy that gained prominence in several
        non-capitalist countries after the 1917 Russian Revolution is
        based on what economic philosophy?
        Socialism

209.   Alexander Pushkin is often considered the father of literature
        of a country that has access to three of the world's oceans—the
        Atlantic, the Arctic, and the Pacific. Name this country.
        Russia

210. The Russian city of Murmansk lies on what peninsula?
Kola Peninsula

211. Name Siberia's largest city.
Novosibirsk

212. A traditional community of predominantly martial people, well known for their horsemanship, lives in the southern steppe regions of Russia and Ukraine. These people are known by what name?
Cossacks

213. The event that involved the violent removal of the Russian Czar in 1917 that was followed by the establishment of a Communist government is known in history by what name?
Russian Revolution

214. The Iraqi city of Mosul is on what river?
Tigris River

215. The 2004 tsunami resulted in extensive ecological damage to Yala National Park and the Hikkaduwa Marine Sanctuary near the city of Galle in what Asian island country?
Sri Lanka

216. The Yellow Sea port of Qingdao is on the southern tip of what Chinese peninsula?
Shandong Peninsula

217. Name the provincial capital of Pakistan's Khyber Pakhtunkhwa Province (formerly North-West Frontier).
Peshawar

218. What Asian megacity lies on the banks of the Sumida River?
Tokyo

219.	Name the world's only two countries that share their borders with fourteen other nations.
China and Russia

220.	In 1930, Mahatma Gandhi led a historic protest known as the Salt March in the coastal village of Dandi in the state of Gujarat in what Asian country?
India

221.	Al-Jees Mountains are located in Ra's Al Khaymah in what country on the Arabian Peninsula?
United Arab Emirates (UAE)

222.	One of the oldest continuously inhabited towns in the world is situated 48 miles east of Mosul, Iraq, and is linked by roads to Turkey, Syria, and Iran. Name this city in the region of Iraqi Kurdistan.
Arbil

223.	The Azadi Tower is the first landmark visitors tend to see when they arrive at the Mehrabad International Airport in what Southwest Asian capital city at the foot of the Elburz Mountains?
Tehran

224.	Leo Tolstoy, the author of *War and Peace* and *Anna Karenina*, hails from what transcontinental country that sent the first human into space?
Russia

225.	Sochi, a city on the Black Sea that was chosen to host the 2014 Olympics, has Europe's most northerly tea plantations. This is a city in what transcontinental country?
Russia

226.	Name the country in mainland Asia that lies directly west of the island of Hainan.
Vietnam

227. Teak is the most valuable export of what Southeast Asian country bordered by China's Yunnan Province?
Myanmar

228. Name the Eurasian country that has been a NATO member since 1952 but does not belong to the European Union?
Turkey

229. The state of Selangor belongs to what Asian country separated into two regions by the South China Sea?
Malaysia

230. Name the country on the coast of the Bay of Bengal that has the world's largest river delta.
Bangladesh

231. Before Japan overran Burma in 1942, the Burma Road, which ran from Lashio, Burma, to Kunming, China, was used by the British to transport arms shipments from Yangon to China. The city of Kunming is the capital of what present-day Chinese province?
Yunnan

232. Sanjay Gandhi National Park, also known as Borivali National Park, is home to more than 1,000 species of plants, 40 species of mammals, and 200 species of birds. This Asian city, on the Arabian Sea coastline, is one of the top metropolises in the world. Name this city.
Mumbai

233. Bharata Natyam and Manipuri are classical dances from what Asian country that is roughly split in two by the Tropic of Cancer?
India

234. Namche Bazar, known for its Tibetan market that sells inexpensive Chinese clothing, is in the Khumbu region of what Asian country?
Nepal

235. Name the Portuguese island colony whose port once dominated the international trade in silk and spices that was returned to China in 1999.
Macau

236. Mount Pinatubo, which erupted in 1991, lies northwest of what bay?
Manila Bay

237. What archipelago separates Borneo from the Philippine island of Mindanao?
Sulu Archipelago

238. What country borders Iran's Kopet-Dag Mountains?
Turkmenistan

239. The largest city in the western half of China, which lies to the northwest of Turpan, is often considered to be the city that is farthest from any sea in the world. Name this city.
Urumqi

240. The Terra Cotta warriors, China's greatest archaeological treasure, are found in what city that was the starting point of the fabled Silk Road?
Xian

241. The multicultural city in Russia that celebrated its 1,000-year anniversary in 2005 has roots in both European and Asian cultures. Name this city on the banks of the Volga River that is the capital of the Republic of Tatarstan.
Kazan

242. The mystical poet Rumi, a Sufi, is often considered the founder of the Mevlevi Order that is sometimes associated with the colorful "whirling dervishes." Most of Rumi's poems were written in what country?
Turkey

243. The Giant Panda Breeding Research Base in Chengdu is an important tourist center in what Chinese province?
Sichuan

244. Mt. Kanchenjunga, India's highest peak, straddles the border of Nepal and what Indian state that has Gangtok as its capital?
Sikkim

245. The historic city of Isfahan is a showcase of the Safavid dynasty. In recent times, a nuclear station, near this city, was the subject of nuclear disagreement between the UN Security Council members and this Asian country. Name this country.
Iran

246. The 5-story salmon-pink Palace of the Winds is a tourist attraction in a city in the historic land of the Rajputs. This city is in India's largest state by area. Name this state.
Rajasthan

247. Name the narrow waterway linking the Black Sea to the Sea of Azov.
Strait of Kerch

248. The Temple of Khajuraho, the product of the creativity of the Chandela kings, was built in 1000 C.E.. This is in what state that, before November 1, 2000, was India's largest state?
Madhya Pradesh

249. The 1942 World War II Battle of Bataan was fought on a peninsula near Luzon Island in what Asian country?
Philippines

250. Joe Rosenthal, the Associated Press photographer, took the famous picture of US soldiers struggling to force the flagpole into the volcanic earth of a mountain during the World War II Battle of Iwo Jima. Name this mountain.
Mount Suribachi

251. The World War II Battle of Corregidor was fought at the entrance of what bay off the Bataan Peninsula?
Manila Bay

252. Three historic battles were fought at Panipat between 1556 and 1761 in the state of Haryana in what Asian country bordering Nepal and Bhutan?
India

253. Even critics believe that, under Ramzan Kadyrov's presidency, the war-torn capital city of a Russian republic that borders the republics of Ingushetia and Dagestan is coming out of the rubble of a long conflict. Name this city.
Grozny (capital of Chechnya)

254. Founded in 1557, what port was the oldest European outpost in China?
Macau

255. In the early 1990s, President Mikhail Gorbachev's policy of glasnost (openness) and perestroika (restructuring) marked the beginning of a capitalist economic movement in what former country?
Soviet Union

256.   In 1900, a secret society called the Boxers led a rebellion to remove all foreigners from its country. Name this Asian country.
China

257.   The 1857 Sepoy Mutiny in the British Army forced the British to bring what Asian country under the Crown?
India

258.   Which Middle Eastern ethnic group was promised autonomy in the Treaty of Sevres (1920), which was never ratified?
Kurds

259.   What Japanese mountain is located at the point where the Eurasian plate, the Okhotsk plate, and the Philippine plate meet?
Mt. Fuji

260.   The Seikan Tunnel, across the Tsugaru Strait, connects the island of Honshu with what major island?
Hokkaido

261.   Name the Japanese city that does not belong and explain why: Kumano, Toyota, Yokohama, Muroto, Oda.
Muroto, because it is not on the island of Honshu; it is in Shikoku

262.   The city of Nara has the Great Buddha Hall of Todaiji that is considered to be one of the world's largest wooden structures. Nara is accessible from Kyoto and what other city that lies at the mouth of the Yodo River?
Osaka

263.   When Buddhism discouraged meat, the Japanese Buddhist population substituted meat with what popular vegetable protein?
Tofu

264.   Name the traditional Japanese type of theater known for the elaborate makeup of its performers who change characters and forms during the course of their performance.
Kabuki

265.   The art of flower arranging, growing of miniature trees, and goldfish breeding are some of the hobbies popular in Japan. What is the popular name for the art of growing miniature trees?
Bonsai

266.   The gateway of a Shinto shrine is known by what name?
Torii

267.   The kimono is the traditional dress of what Asian country?
Japan

268.   What small peninsula juts out of Honshu into the Pacific just south of Mt. Fuji and southeast of the city of Yokohama?
Izu Peninsula

269.   Which Japanese island is bitterly cold in winter and has harsh volcanic mountains?
Hokkaido

270.   In 1854, Commodore Perry arrived in Tokyo paving the way for opening up Japan to the West. Tokyo was known by what name during that period?
Edo

271.   The Caspian Gates are located in Derbent, the southernmost city in Russia, comprise a narrow strip of land that forms a natural pass between the Caucasus and the Caspian Sea. This pass is in what Russian republic?
Dagestan

272.   The Harirud River flows from Afghanistan into Turkmenistan,
        where it disappears into the Kara-Kum desert. Name the
        northwestern province in Afghanistan that borders Turkmenistan
        and lies in the valley of the Harirud River.
        Herat

273.   What river in central Asia was once known as the Jaxartes River?
        Syr Darya

274.   A state, on the west coast of India that used to be the starting
        point for Muslim pilgrims to Mecca later became the capital of
        the Portuguese Empire in the East. Name this state.
        Goa

275.   In 1501, Portuguese explorer Pedro Alvares Cabral sailed to the
        cities of Calicut and Cochin in the state of Kerala in what Asian
        country?
        India

276.   In 1896, the Mongol emperor Kublai Khan's fleet was decimated by
        hurricanes as it invaded what Asian island country, east of China?
        Japan

277.   Vietnam's Red River originates in what Chinese province?
        Yunnan

278.   The town of Kashi in China, on the Silk Road, is known by what
        modern name?
        Kashgar

279.   The Wolesi Jirga is the lower house of the National Assembly
        of a mountainous Asian country that has Farah as one of its
        westernmost provinces. Name this country.
        Afghanistan

280. Dujail is a Shiite town 40 miles north of what Iraqi city?
Baghdad

281. The Al-Askari mosque, a revered Shiite shrine on the east bank of
the Tigris River, is in what Iraqi city?
Samarra

282. Iriomote Jima is a mountainous island at the southern end of
an archipelago that stretches from Taiwan to Japan. Name this
archipelago.
Ryukyu

283. The Kallang-Paya Lebar Expressway, presumably the longest
subterranean road tunnel in Southeast Asia, is in what island
nation near the southern tip of the Malay Peninsula?
Singapore

284. The Chinese city of Tianjin lies on what gulf?
Bohai Gulf

285. What Chinese city, located west of the Yellow Sea and east of the
Bohai Sea, is now a major center of IT industry at the southern
end of the Liaodong Peninsula?
Dalian

286. The holy city of Benares, also known as Varanasi, is in India's
most populous state. Name this state.
Uttar Pradesh

287. In 1907, explorer Sir Aurel Stein visited a place of pilgrimage
in Dunhuang, China. Known for the "Caves of the Thousand
Buddhas," this city is near the western end of what desert?
Gobi Desert

288. The city of Andijan is in which Central Asian country?
Uzbekistan

289. In 1558, an expedition led by Anthony Jenkinson, a Portuguese monarch, was provided a safe passage by the Russian Czar Ivan IV to Astrakhan via Kazan and the Volga. Astrakhan is a major port located in the delta of what river about 60 miles from the Caspian Sea?
Volga River

290. The World War II Battle of the Leyte Gulf was fought in what country?
Philippines

291. A historic World War II battle was fought on October 24, 1944, in what body of water north of Panay Island in the Philippines?
Sibuyan Sea

292. Name the most populous island in the world that was the center of powerful Hindu kingdoms and of the colonial Dutch East Indies.
Java

293. The Tarawa Atoll is part of what island chain?
Gilbert Islands

294. The World War II Battle of the Coral Sea was fought in the waters southwest of what islands?
Solomon Islands

295. The island of Saipan is part of what larger island group?
Northern Mariana Islands

296. In 1989, the military junta changed the name of Burma to Myanmar. Although accepted by the United Nations, what two countries still officially refer to it by its old name?
USA and the UK

297. The Jiaozhou Bay bridge, considered to be the world's longest bridge over water, links China's port city of Qingdao to the offshore island of Huangdao. Qingdao is on the southern coastline of what peninsula in eastern China between Bo Hai and the Yellow Sea?
Shandong Peninsula

298. According to reports, the world's largest democracy is also the third-largest economy in terms of purchasing power. Name this country.
India

299. Name the second-largest city in Burma which is often considered the cultural capital of the country.
Mandalay

300. The ancient city of Taxila was influenced by Persia, Greece, and central Asia. From the 5th century B.C.E. to the 2nd century C.E., this city was an important Buddhist center of learning in the second most populous country with a Muslim majority. Name this country.
Pakistan

301. What line, named after an explorer who identified the division between Asian and Australian types of flora and fauna, supports the theory that the western and eastern islands of the Malay/Indonesian archipelago (from Malaysia to New Guinea) formed parts of separate continents?
Wallace Line

302. Name Pakistan's most populous province.
Punjab

303. In October 2007, Canada granted honorary citizenship to pro-democracy activist Aung San Suu Kyi. This Nobel laureate is from what Asian country that borders Bangladesh?
Myanmar

304. Name the country, with Eilat Bay at its southern tip, that consists of mainly three geographic regions—the coastal plain, the mountain region, and the Jordan Rift Valley.
Israel

305. Badaling Hills, one of the most impressive and best-preserved sections of the fabled Great Wall of China, is near what Chinese city?
Beijing

306. In the 23rd century B.C.E., the Egyptian explorer Harkhuf was sent to find a road to Yam, which is now known by what name?
China

307. Name Thailand's largest island.
Phuket

308. Name the island between Borneo and the Moluccas that was formerly known as Celebes.
Sulawesi

309. Name the largest island of the Nagasaki prefecture that has the same name as a channel belonging to the Korea Strait.
Tsushima

310. Militant hideouts in the town of Zhob in the Baluchistan province have been a serious concern for the government of what Asian country?
Pakistan

311. Shanghai, China's most populated city, was opened to foreign trade by what treaty in 1842?
Treaty of Nanking

312. The Id Kah Mosque, the largest Islamic mosque in China, was built in an oasis city in the western part of the country. Name this city that is located on the legendary Silk Road in the Xinjiang region.
Kashgar

313. Name the Russian island, once a rocket-launching site, situated to the north of Novaya Zemlya and east of Svalbard?
Franz Josef Land

314. The Black Sea region of Krasnodar is in what transcontinental country?
Russia

315. The volcanic mountains of Makiling, Banahaw, and San Cristobal are found 50 miles south of what southeastern Asian capital city?
Manila

316. Mt. Hermon is the highest peak and the only skiing site of what southwestern Asian nation?
Israel

317. What is the capital of the autonomous Kurdish region in Iraq?
Arbil

318. Congress is to the United States as Diet is to what?
Japan

319. What is the capital of Abkhazia, an autonomous region of northwestern Georgia?
Sukhumi

320. Niigata prefecture is in the Chubu Region of what Asian country?
Japan

321.   Name Asia's largest desert.
Gobi Desert

322.   Masada, the place where Jewish fighters took refuge after the
fall of Jerusalem in 74 C.E., is a fortress located at the top of
an isolated rock on the edge of the Judean desert. This fortress
overlooks what valley in Israel?
Dead Sea Valley

323.   The Shiite Muslims, the Sunni Muslims, and what other religious
group comprise the three main religious groups in Iraq?
Christian

324.   Basho's Trail is a holy pilgrimage route on what Japanese island?
Honshu

325.   Name the Indian city in the state of Andhra Pradesh that has the
same name as a former capital of the Sindh province in Pakistan.
Hyderabad

326.   The Lower House in Russia is known by what name?
State Duma

327.   Kolkata, the capital of the Indian state of West Bengal, is situated
on the banks of what river?
Hooghly River

328.   Name the small mountainous kingdom bordering India and China.
Bhutan

329.   The province of Nghe An is bordered by the Asian nation of Laos
to the west. Name the country where this province is located.
Vietnam

330. The Moro Islamic Liberation Front is located on the easternmost major island in the Philippines. Name this island.
Mindanao

331. Garagum Desert dominates what country?
Turkmenistan

332. Name the largest port city located in the Primorsky Krai, a province that Russia acquired from China by the Treaty of Aigun in 1858.
Vladivostok

333. Name the Asian country with the marshy Rann of Kutch to its west.
India

334. Name Israel's southernmost city.
Eilat

335. The Isthmus of Kra connects the Malay Peninsula with mainland Asia. This isthmus is shared by which two countries?
Thailand and Myanmar (Burma)

336. The port city of Tyre is in what country?
Lebanon

337. The Hebei Province is located in what Asian country?
China

338. What is the name of the desert-dwelling nomadic Arabs?
Bedouin

339. Name the Mediterranean strip of land that has Rafah as its largest city on its Egyptian border.
Gaza Strip

340.   The Knesset is the parliamentary body of what Middle Eastern
       country?
       Israel

341.   What large Asian country has only one time zone despite its size?
       China

342.   Name the island country that has the Kanto Plain as its largest
       lowland area.
       Japan

343.   What Asian country has Hai Phong as one of its major seaports on
       the Red River delta?
       Vietnam

344.   Name the Middle Eastern city that was once the center of a
       Phoenician confederation that included the cities of Tyre, Sidon,
       and Arados.
       Tripoli

345.   Cosmonauts are to Russia as Taikonauts are to what?
       China

346.   Name the Middle Eastern capital city in the Ghouta region that
       lies along the Barada River.
       Damascus

347.   What Chinese administrative unit is located on the Pearl River
       Delta, south of Guangdong Province?
       Hong Kong

348.   Name the East Asian country, directly south of Taiwan, whose
       famous and ancient Banaue Rice Terraces are a UNESCO World
       Heritage Site.
       Philippines

349. The northeastern state of Tripura is in what Asian country
      bordering Nepal and Pakistan?
      India

350. Baghdad is on what river?
      Tigris River

351. What country is bordered by Kazakhstan to the north and China
      to the east?
      Kyrgyzstan

352. The Tenzing-Hillary Airport is located at Lukla in what Asian
      country?
      Nepal

353. What country, the smallest in Asia by area and population, is
      about 435 miles southwest of Sri Lanka?
      Maldives

354. Name the special territory of Indonesia located at the northern tip
      of Sumatra.
      Aceh

355. Name the Russian republic whose capital is Grozny.
      Chechnya

356. What Arab country has Ajman as one of its Emirates and uses the
      Emirati Dirham?
      United Arab Emirates

357. What mainland country is located to the east of the Strait of Malacca?
      Malaysia

358. What country borders Kazakhstan, China, and Tajikistan?
      Kyrgyzstan

359. The town of Jask is located about 1,050 miles south of Tehran along the coast of what gulf?
Gulf of Oman

360. What island in northwestern Sri Lanka has the same name as a gulf in the area?
Mannar Island

361. What is the Arabian country that has Socotra as its largest island?
Yemen

362. What Chinese province has the source of three major rivers, the Yellow River, the Mekong River, and the Yangtze River?
Qinghai

363. The region of Kurdistan is located between Iraq and what country?
Turkey

364. Give the present-day name of India's largest city.
Mumbai

365. Name the smallest Asian country in terms of area and population.
Maldives

366. Name the Russian city at the mouth of the Neva River on the Baltic Sea.
St. Petersburg

367. The republic of Ingushetia is in which country?
Russia

368. Name the second-largest city of Philippines.
Manila

369. Name the Asian country that has Chiang Mai as its second-largest province.
Thailand

370. What Japanese island is separated from Shikoku by the Bungo Channel?
Kyushu

371. What Asian capital is located on the Chao Phraya River?
Bangkok

372. What is the most populated city in the Arab world?
Cairo

373. Name the country where Bengali is the most widely spoken language.
Bangladesh

374. The city of Wattala is in what Asian island country that was once known to Greek geographers as Taprobane?
Sri Lanka

375. Name the second-largest city in Afghanistan, which is also its major Pashto-speaking city.
Kandahar

376. Assam, a state in India's northeastern region, is located on which river?
Brahmaputra

377. Name the de facto independent republic in northwestern Georgia.
Abkhazia

378. Ternate is a town in the Molucca Islands in the eastern part of what Asian country?
Indonesia

379. The highly populous city of Perm is an administrative center in the Perm Krai on the banks of the Kama River in what country?
Russia
(Note: In Russia, *krais* were historically vast territories located along the periphery of the country. Currently, however, the usage of the term is mostly traditional as some oblasts also fit this description and there is no difference in legal status between the *krais* and the *oblasts*. In the Soviet Union (according to its Constitution of 1977, Ch.11), the only difference between *krais* and *oblasts* were that an autonomous *oblast* could be a sub-division of a *krai* or of a union republic, but not of an *oblast*. Russia did not save this difference.)

380. The Kosi River, which flows through India and Nepal, is one of the largest tributaries of what major river?
Ganges River

381. Trincomalee is located northeast of Kandy in what island country in Asia?
Sri Lanka

382. Name the Asian country that has Ishikari as one of its longest rivers.
Japan

383. What is the largest province in Iraq?
Al Anbar (or Anbar)

384. Name the Asian country dominated by the Khorat Plateau bordered by the Mekong River to its east.
Thailand

385. The Waziristan region is in what Asian country that is located east of Iran?
Pakistan

386.   Name the Asian country separated from Tajikistan by the narrow
       Wakhan Corridor.
       Pakistan

387.   The airport hub of Hat Yai is located near which country's
       southern border with Malaysia?
       Thailand

388.   The Ha Giang province contains the northernmost point of an
       Asian country on its border with China. Name this country.
       Vietnam

389.   The Sichuan Province is in what country whose capital is home to
       the Forbidden City?
       China

390.   The Lampung Province is located in the world's largest
       archipelagic country. Name this country.
       Indonesia

391.   The city of Khost was the first city that was liberated from
       Communist rule during the Soviet invasion of which country in
       the 1980s?
       Afghanistan

392.   What region, the only one in the Philippines that has its own
       government, is composed of predominantly Muslim provinces?
       Mindanao

393.   What large Asian country has the world's fastest-growing
       economy?
       China

394.   Central Anatolia's Konya Province is in what secular democratic
       country?
       Turkey

395. Name the largest city, located on the banks of the Sabarmati River, in the Indian state that extends farthest west.
Ahmedabad (in Gujarat)

396. Name Turkey's largest city, the second largest metropolitan area in Europe and home to the Hagia Sophia.
Istanbul

397. Name the city that lies on the site of the ancient Assyrian city of Arrapha and is the center of the northern Iraqi petroleum industry.
Kirkuk

398. Name the Japanese island that is home to the Osaka-Kobe-Kyoto megalopolis.
Honshu

399. India's third most populous city, known as the Silicon Valley of India, is located on the Deccan Plateau. Name this city.
Bengaluru (Bangalore)

400. Name the Asian city on the island of Luzon whose metropolitan area is divided by the Pasig River.
Manila

401. One of Asia's youngest republics, whose flag is pennant-shaped, was a Hindu monarchy until May 2008. Name this country.
Nepal

402. Kunming is the capital of Yunnan Province in what country that largely speaks Mandarin?
China

403. The Khmer Temple of Prasat Preah Vihear is a UNESCO World Heritage site located on the border of what two Southeast Asian nations?
Cambodia and Thailand

404.   Russia peacefully shares the disputed regions along the Argun, the
        Ussuri, and the Amur Rivers with which country to its south?
        China

405.   What country that has the cities of Ansan and Cheongju
        administers the Dokdo Islands?
        South Korea

406.   The Kamchatka Peninsula is part of what region that comprises
        almost 77% of Russia's land area?
        Siberia

407.   The city of Toyako, named after the nearby Lake Toya, is located
        on what Japanese island?
        Hokkaido

408.   Name the strategically situated rocky plateau in southwestern
        Syria, located at the southern end of the Anti-Lebanon Mountains.
        Golan Heights

409.   China and which other country that owns the Bonin Islands share
        ownership of the Chunxiao gas field in a disputed area of the East
        China Sea?
        Japan

410.   Name the Middle Eastern federation of seven sheikdoms that uses
        the dirham.
        United Arab Emirates

411.   The city of Baqubah lies on the Diyala River in what Middle
        Eastern country?
        Iraq

412.   Cox's Bazar is known for one of the world's longest natural sand
        beaches and is situated to the south of the city of Chittagong in
        what country?
        Bangladesh

413.   Mindanao is an autonomous region in which Asian country that is
        predominantly Christian?
        Philippines

414.   The Kandahar province can be found in what Asian country on
        Pakistan's western border?
        Afghanistan

415.   What large Asian country launched the East Turkestan Islamic
        Movement to counteract the efforts a rebel group in its Uyghur
        Autonomous Region?
        China

416.   Tskhinvali is the capital of what disputed Georgian territory?
        South Ossetia

417.   The Turkish town of Bandirma is on the coast of what body of
        water that is connected to the Black Sea through the Bosporus and
        to the Aegean Sea through the Dardanelles Strait?
        Sea of Marmara

418.   The Roki Tunnel, a mountain tunnel, connects Georgia's
        breakaway republic of South Ossetia with what Russian republic?
        North Ossetia

419.   Located at the confluence of the Varzob and the Kofarnihon
        Rivers, what is the largest city in Tajikistan?
        Dushanbe

420.   Name the transcontinental country in the Caucasus that contains
        the republics of South Ossetia and Abkhazia.
        Georgia

421.   Known as the Shanghai Five before the addition of Uzbekistan,
        the Shanghai Cooperation Organization (SCO), a mutual-security
        organization, includes China, Kazakhstan, Kyrgyzstan, Tajikistan,
        Uzbekistan, and what large country?
        Russia

422.   What Black Sea port in Georgia is located about 12 miles from
        the Turkish border?
        Batumi

423.   The town of Gori, the birthplace of Joseph Stalin, is located in
        what small Caucasian country?
        Georgia

424.   One of the world's longest pipelines, the BTC pipeline, connects
        Baku, Tbilisi, and a port on Turkey's southern coast on the
        Mediterranean. Name this city.
        Ceyhan

425.   What does SAARC, an economic and political organization of
        eight southern Asian countries, stand for?
        South Asian Association for Regional Cooperation

426.   An attack on a police post in Kashgar, in China's largest political
        subdivision, disrupted peace in this autonomous region.
        Xinjiang Uyghur

427.   The Georgian port city of Poti, near the ancient Greek colony of
        Phasis, lies on the coast of what body of water?
        Black Sea

CHAPTER 7

Australia, Antarctica, and the Pacific

1. Name the South Pacific country about 1,300 miles north of
    Auckland, New Zealand, located east of Vanuatu and west of
    Tonga, which gained independence from Great Britain in 1970.
    Fiji

2. Captain Cook's Beach, located on the Coromandel Peninsula, is
    located in what Polynesian island country?
    New Zealand

3. Botany Bay, explorer James Cook's landing site, is near what
    Australian city?
    Sydney, New South Wales

4. Which Australian state, known for its wine-producing Barossa
    Valley, became the first state to give its Aborigines their land rights?
    South Australia

5. The site of the first European colony in Australia, established in
    1788, is near what major Australian city?
    Sydney

6. Name the westernmost Australian capital.
    Perth

7. Whale Shark viewing is an attraction in an Australian city on the
    Indian Ocean at the tip of North West Cape. Name this city.
    Exmouth

8. Which Australian state capital lies on the Swan River?
    Perth

9. Name the independent archipelago in the South Pacific that
    is often known as the Friendly Islands because of the friendly
    welcome Captain Cook received when he landed there.
    Tonga

10. The formation of limestone stacks, known as the Twelve Apostles, is an attraction in what state on the southern coast of Australia?
Victoria

11. What ice shelf, near the western part of Antarctica at the edge of the Weddell Sea, is considered by many as the second-largest body of floating ice in the world?
Ronne Ice Shelf

12. The Gondwana Rainforests are situated on the Great Escarpment on the east coast of what country?
Australia

13. The Taiaroa Peninsula is in what country in the Southern Hemisphere that added Stewart Island as its newest national park?
New Zealand

14. Moorea is among the many islands discovered by the Polynesians about 1,400 years ago. This is near what island in French Polynesia?
Tahiti

15. Kangaroo Island is a remarkable haven for native wildlife in what Australian state?
South Australia

16. Name the Australian mountain ranges in South Australia that stretch from north of St. Vincent's Gulf far into the Australian outback.
Flinders Ranges

17. Quorn, an important railway town in the 19th century, is situated in an Australian state that has the Yorke and the Eyre peninsulas. Name this state.
South Australia

18.   Animal lovers often enjoy the sight of killer cane toads near the capital city of Australia's Northern Territories. Name this city.
Darwin

19.   Kiwi is the national bird of what country in the Southern Hemisphere?
New Zealand

20.   What is the name of the most populous city in the Australian island state of Tasmania, lying on the Derwent River?
Hobart

21.   Dromedaries, one-humped camels, are the only camels found in the deserts of what country in the Southern Hemisphere?
Australia

22.   You can often find aboriginal rock paintings when traveling to what famous national park in Australia's Northern Territory?
Kakadu National Park

23.   Which of these places in New Zealand is furthest north?
Abel Tasman National Park, Wellington, Arthur's Pass National Park, Mt. Cook
Abel Tasman National Park

24.   Ayers Rock, Kakadu National Park, and the city of Darwin lie in what Australian administrative region?
Northern Territory

25.   In what country in Polynesia would you cross the Canterbury Plains to see the mighty Franz Josef Glacier?
New Zealand

26.   The Isle of the Dead, originally called Opossum Island, may have one of the earliest benchmarks in the world for scientific measurement of changes in sea level and for studying global warming. This isle is located in the harbor adjacent to Port Arthur in what large island in the Southern Hemisphere?
Tasmania

27.   Tauranga is the largest city on the Bay of Plenty in what Pacific island country that has Chatham Islands as one of its territories?
New Zealand

28.   Most of the Murray-Darling river system lies in what Australian state?
New South Wales

29.   The Dronning Maud Land in Antarctica is a dependency of what European country?
Norway

30.   Name the world's largest sandstone monolith.
Ayers Rock

31.   Saipan, which was under Japanese control during WWII, is the largest city on what US territorial islands?
Northern Mariana Islands

32.   Name the country that has the second-largest sub-national entity in the world after the Sakha Republic in Russia. Name this entity.
Australia (state of Western Australia)

33.   The Santa Cruz Islands are part of what nation in Melanesia that lies east of Papua New Guinea and is well known for the World War II Battle of Guadalcanal?
Solomon Islands

34. Watarrka National Park and Kings Canyon are in what Australian administrative unit to the west of Queensland?
Northern Territory

35. Kwajalein (Kwajalong), the largest atoll in the world, surrounds a 655-square-mile lagoon. This coral formation is in the Ralik Chain of what republic in the western Pacific Ocean?
Marshall Islands

36. Name the nearest US island territory to the north of the Marshall Islands.
Wake Island

37. Tepuka is one of the islets circling a large lagoon in what atoll in Tuvalu?
Funafuti Atoll

38. What Polynesian island group that consists of the Nuka Hiva, Ua Pou, and Ua Huka islands was made famous by James Cook, novelist Herman Melville, and painter Paul Gauguin?
Marquesas Islands

39. The triangular geographical region formed by the Hawaiian Islands, New Zealand, and Easter Island is often known by what name?
Polynesia
(Note: Midway Atoll could be considered as one of the points in this triangle. The Polynesian Cultural Center in Oahu defines Hawaii as one of the three points and so do other resources.)

40. The land of what is now Bungle Bungle National Park, also called the Purnululu National Park, was created at the same time as most of the Kimberley scenery around 350 million years ago. This park is in what Australian state?
Western Australia

41. Name the large country that lies to the southwest of the Solomon Islands, Vanuatu, and New Caledonia.
Australia

42. Exmouth, Australia, once a US Navy town, provides easy access to Ningaloo Reef, Cape Range National Park, and the pristine Turquoise Bay. Exmouth is on the coast of what body of water?
Indian Ocean

43. The Foveaux Strait separates South Island (New Zealand) from what other island?
Stewart Island

44. Name the item that does not belong and explain why: Nauru, Niue, Cook Islands.
Nauru, because it lies west of the International Date Line
(Note: Prior to 1994, the western and the eastern islands of Kiribati were on either side of the International Date Line. In 1994, the president of Kiribati moved the date line for convenience, thereby bringing all the islands to the west of the International Date Line. Nauru is also not a territory of New Zealand. Depending on the way the question is framed, there could be two ways to single out the item from this list.)

45. Name the item that does not belong and explain why: Midway Islands, Johnson Atoll, Tokelau, Wake Island.
Tokelau, because it belongs to New Zealand; the others belong to the United States

46. What is the name of the basin that extends from the state of South Australia to Queensland?
Great Artesian Basin

47. Phillip Island in Australia is known for its fairy penguins. This island belongs to what state?
Victoria

48.   The city of Gold Coast in Queensland, Australia, is situated on
      what ocean?
      Pacific Ocean

49.   What city in the Australian state of New South Wales is on the
      Hunter River?
      Newcastle

50.   Name the body of water that lies between the Antarctic Peninsula
      and Dronning Maud Land.
      Weddell Sea

51.   Great Sandy National Park lies on the northern half of the world's
      largest sand island. Name this island.
      Fraser Island

52.   The Shackleton Ice Shelf is situated on what body of water off the
      coast of Wilkes Land in Antarctica?
      Indian Ocean

53.   In 1983, the world's lowest air temperature was recorded at
      a Russian scientific research station in Antarctica. Name this
      station.
      Vostok

54.   What is the name of the sea along the west side of the Antarctic
      Peninsula that lies between Alexander Island and Thurston
      Island?
      Bellinghausen Sea

55.   Name the region that is situated entirely within the Antarctic
      Circle. Wilkes Land, Enderby Land, Antarctic Peninsula, Marie
      Byrd Land
      Marie Byrd Land

56. Using the equator as a reference point, name the item that does not belong and explain why: Fiji, Solomon Islands, Marshall Islands, Vanuatu.
Marshall Islands, because it is the only one in the group that lies to the north of the equator

57. Mount Isa is in what Australian state that borders South Australia and New South Wales?
Queensland

58. Australia's Eyre Peninsula is bounded by what gulf to its east?
Spencer Gulf

59. The Darling Range is in what Australian state?
Western Australia

60. Name Australia's largest state by area.
Western Australia

61. Tokelau is a territory of what South Pacific country in Polynesia?
New Zealand

62. The Three Kings Islands lie to the northwest of what major island of New Zealand?
North Island

63. Name the body of water that does not belong and explain why: Tasman Bay, Hawke Bay, Bay of Plenty, and South Taranaki Bight.
Tasman Bay, because it is on New Zealand's South Island; the others are on the North Island

64. The uninhabited Starbuck Island belongs to a collection of eleven atolls in Micronesia, eight of which belong to Kiribati. Name this island chain.
Line Islands

65. The US Amundsen-Scott research station is located at what point in Antarctica?
South Pole or Geographic South Pole
(Note: Magnetic South Pole is incorrect)

66. Yapese is an Austronesian language spoken by people on an island in what Pacific Ocean nation?
Federated States of Micronesia

67. Nan Madol, the ancient social, political, and religious center of the Saudeleur dynasty, was built on Temwen Island. This island is part of what larger Micronesian island group?
Pohnpei

68. Name the Pacific Ocean nation that has Palikir as its capital.
Federated States of Micronesia

69. What country borders the Indonesian province of Papua?
Papua New Guinea

70. Name the Micronesian nation in the Northern Hemisphere, just west of the International Date Line and south of Wake Island.
Marshall Islands

71. Name the South Pacific island nation with Espiritu Santo as its largest island.
Vanuatu

72. Majuro is the largest city in what Pacific island nation?
Marshall Islands

73. Bougainville is an autonomous region in what country that shares New Guinea with Indonesia?
Papua New Guinea

74. Name the Melanesian Pidgin-speaking country that has a large wetland along its Sepik and Fly Rivers.
Papua New Guinea

75. Aborigines control 80% of the coast of what Australian political unit that is famous for its Kakadu National Park?
Northern Territory

76. The only sovereign monarchy among the island nations of the Pacific Ocean uses the paanga as its currency. Name this country.
Tonga

77. What Pacific Ocean island is named after the Cornish explorer Samuel Wallis?
Wallis Island

78. Name the largest city in Australia, which is built around Port Jackson, the site of the country's first European settlement.
Sydney

79. What self-governing parliamentary democracy is in free association with New Zealand and is sometimes known as the Rock of Polynesia?
Niue

80. What Australian coastal capital city is located east of Gulf St. Vincent and to the north of the Fleurieu Peninsula?
Adelaide

81. Name the largest and southernmost of the Mariana Islands whose indigenous people are known as Chamorros.
Guam

82. What Pacific country's independence was established by the Treaty of Waitangi in 1840?
New Zealand

83. Most of the people of the Northern Mariana Islands are of mixed Micronesian and Spanish ancestry. Name these people.
Chamorros

84. The Garig Gunak Barlu National Park encompasses most of what peninsula that occupies the western tip of Arnhem Land?
Cobourg Peninsula

85. The largest settlement on the Nullarbor Plain is also the easternmost settlement in Western Australia. Name this settlement on the Great Australian Bight.
Eucla

86. Mt. Minto is a mostly ice-free mountain in the Admiralty Mountains that was discovered by Capt. James Ross in January 1841. This is the highest mountain in what Antarctic region?
Victoria Land

87. Gore, located on the Mataura River, is the second-largest town in New Zealand's southernmost region that includes Stewart Island. Name this region.
Southland

88. The Vatu-i-ra Channel separates the two biggest islands of which Pacific Ocean country?
Fiji

89. The Shotover Jet operates one of the world's most exciting jet boat rides in the Shotover River Canyons near Queenstown in the Otago region of which country?
New Zealand

90. Name the largest village on the island of Tinian in the Northern Mariana Islands.
San Jose

91. Lake Taupo is on which of New Zealand's islands?
North Island

92. Ambrym Volcano is one of the most active volcanoes in the region of Oceania. This is in what country to the southeast of Solomon Islands?
Vanuatu

93. Most of the residents of Solomon Islands are what—Melanesians or Polynesians?
Melanesians

94. Ducie Island, in the South Pacific, belongs to which European country?
United Kingdom

95. The Australian city of Mildura lies just to the southeast of the confluence of which two rivers?
Murray and Darling Rivers

96. In 1616, a Dutchman called Dirk Hartog was the first recorded European to land in Western Australia, on an island that is now named after him. This island is just south of Steep Point, Australia's westernmost point in the mainland located within what World Heritage site?
Shark Bay World Heritage Site

97. The basin that feeds the northernmost headwaters of the Darling River originates in which Australian state?
Queensland

98. Name the large body of water off the coast of the Australia's Northern Territory and the state of Western Australia that is also an inlet of Timor Sea.
Joseph Bonaparte Gulf

99.   Name the peninsula in New Zealand located east of the city of Napier and Hawke Bay.

Mahia Peninsula

100.   Name the largest ice shelf in Antarctica.

Ross Ice Shelf

CHAPTER 8

Physical Geography

1. Name the method of age determination based upon the decay of radiocarbon to nitrogen.
   Carbon dating (radiocarbon dating and radioactive carbon dating are acceptable)

2. What term describes a large geographical area of distinctive plant groups, animal groups, and climate that are adapted to that particular environment?
   Biome

3. What is the scientific name of the most recent geologic period in Earth's history when human activities started having a significant impact on climate and ecosystems?
   Anthropocene

4. Ecologists often classify forests by their elevation zone. How are forests that begin at about 1,500-2,000 feet and transition into subalpine forests at about 4,000 feet classified—as Lowland Forests or as Montane Forests?
   Montane Forests

5. What type of forests, which occur between 50 and 60 degrees north latitudes, represent the largest terrestrial biome-Boreal Forests (Taiga) or Temperate Forests?
   Boreal Forests

6. On what type of map projection would you find all lines of latitude drawn as straight lines while all lines of longitude other than the prime meridian are curved?
   Robinson projection

7. Which is made by projecting a globe onto a cylinder that touches Earth's surface along the Equator—an Azimuthal Map Projection or a Mercator Projection?
   Mercator Projection

8. A line that connects areas on a map that have the same elevation is known by what term?
Contour line

9. Using wind speed as a reference, put in order from highest to lowest: storm, breeze, hurricane, gale
Hurricane, storm, gale, breeze

10. What is the name for a lake that is alkaline because of large amount of carbonates?
Soda Lake

11. Contour maps give a picture of the shape of earth. A variation in elevation in a contour map is known by what term?
Relief

12. A weather phenomenon, such a snowfall or storm, influenced by a region's proximity to large lakes, is known by what term?
Lake-effect snow or storm

13. A layer of lake water, located between the warm top layer and the stratified cool and dense lower layer, is known by what term?
Thermocline

14. An underground layer of porous rock that holds water and carries it to springs and wells is an important source of irrigation in the arid regions of the Middle East. These sources are known by what hydrological name?
Aquifers

15. A basin in the desert that has the remains of a mineral crust of salt due to evaporation of water is known by what term?
Salt pan

16.   What is the term for a process where algae growth, initiated by
       rich nutrients, is followed by a die-off and bacterial decomposition
       of the algae that depletes the water's oxygen?
       Eutrophication

17.   A fault block that has been lowered relative to the blocks on
       either side is known by what term?
       Graben (rift valley acceptable)

18.   Often associated with geothermal activity, what geological term
       describes a vent discharging gas and steam in a volcanic region?
       Fumarole

19.   What term describes a bend or a flexure in a rock?
       Fold

20.   What is a geological term for a fold in the rocks of the Earth's
       crust in which the layers or beds dip inward, thus forming a
       trough-like structure with a sag in the middle?
       Syncline

21.   What is the geological term for a fold in the rocks in which the
       layers or beds arch upward?
       Anticline

22.   When a fold where both limbs are almost horizontal, what type of
       fold do we have- monocline or anticline?
       Monocline

23.   A sudden downward movement of snow, ice, and debris in a
       mountainous area is known by what term?
       Avalanche

24. Solifluction is the slow downward movement of a water-saturated component activated by the thawing of permafrost during the brief summers of Earth's Polar Regions. Name this water-saturated component.
Soil

25. The K-T boundary (Cretaceous and Tertiary boundary) event refers to the mass extinction that happened, about 65 million years ago, because of the collision of an asteroid with the Earth. Which of these two periods was first—Cretaceous or Tertiary?
Tertiary

26. At Pamukkale, Turkey, water reaches the surface as hot springs. When minerals in the water form precipitate, they become solid terraces. What type of water, with a high concentration of calcium and magnesium, is needed for this to occur?
Hard water

27. What term describes a fracture in rock?
Fissure

28. Flat areas of the ocean floor that lie at the base of the continental rise are known by what geographic term?
Abyssal Plains

29. An isolated hill usually capped with a layer of rock that often represents remnants of a former extensive slope is known by what term?
Butte or Mesa (Mesas have much larger tops. Buttes are smaller in size.)

30. What causes the two tidal bulges of ocean water—the gravitational effect of the Moon or Earth's topography?
Gravitational effect of the Moon

31. Gravity in the Earth-Moon system and what other factor define tides—the Earth's spin or ocean topography?
Earth's spin

32. The lower boundary of the Earth's crust is named after a discoverer who found a discontinuity in that region. What is this called— Moho or Koppen?
Mohorovicic Discontinuity (Moho)

33. Energy released by subduction of oceanic crust tends to melt mantle rocks. In places like Java, Indonesia, this can result in curved chains of what geological features?
Island volcanoes

34. What is the term that describes a large expanse of sand dunes within a desert?
Erg

35. A tall column of rock rising out of the sea near a coastline is known by what name?
Sea stack

36. A mountain ridge that is cut off and projects downward from the crests of mountains is known by what term?
Spur

37. Name the grid system used by the United States for military map projections between latitudes 80 degrees north and 80 degrees south.
UTM Grid (Universal Transverse Mercator Grid System)

38. A peninsula of sand projecting from a shore where the coastline changes direction is known by what name?
Spit

39.   What biome describes a forest of tall trees in a region that receives more of the sun's energy than the rest of the earth, experiences heavy rainfall, and has a fairly constant temperature throughout the year?
Tropical rainforest

40.   Olympic National Park is an example of what type of rain forest?
Temperate rainforest

41.   What is the thin, rich layer of soil that contains humus and other organisms that make it fertile?
Topsoil

42.   Oceanic crust is made mostly of what type of rock?
Basalt

43.   Hurricane Katrina gathered strength when it passed over what warm ocean current in the Gulf of Mexico that flows northward between Cuba and the Yucatán Peninsula and then into the Gulf of Mexico?
Loop Current

44.   The only penguins that could cross into the Northern Hemisphere can be found on the Galapagos Islands. They were brought to the Galapagos Islands by what ocean current that brings cold waters and nutrients north from Antarctica?
Humboldt Current (Peru Current)

45.   Forests that occur in cold nutrient-rich water that are among the most beautiful and biologically productive habitats in the marine environment are known by what name?
Kelp forests

46.   Hygrometers are used in the measurement of what characteristic of the atmosphere?
Humidity

47. A floating mass of vegetation that has separated from neighboring swamps often blocks the main channels of the White Nile in South Sudan. This type of floating mass is known by what name?
Sudd

48. Ocean current systems of planetary scale driven by the global wind system is known by what name in the glossary of the American Meteorological Society?
Gyres

49. What is the main reason why the Arctic region has drastic day and night cycles?
Earth's tilt

50. Permafrost is a characteristic of what biome between the taiga and the polar desert?
Arctic tundra

51. A plant that grows in dry conditions where water is often limited is known by what name?
Xerophyte

52. A line encircling Antarctica where the cold, northward-flowing, Antarctic waters sink beneath the relatively warmer waters of the sub-Antarctic is known by what name?
Antarctic Convergence

53. This biome that ranges from wastelands to wild gardens is characterized by extremes of climate (high temperatures and summer droughts) and is commonly known by what term in the western United States?
Chaparral (outside of the Western US, Doñana National Park in Spain is another example)

54. Icebergs from western Greenland are known to travel as far south as 40 degrees north. This movement is facilitated by the cold water of what ocean current?
Labrador Current

55. What biome describes large, rolling terrain of grasses, flowers, and herbs?
Grassland

56. A broad, dome-shaped volcanic cone with very gentle slopes and an extensive circumference that fits the characteristics of Mauna Loa, the world's largest volcano, is an example of what type of volcano?
Shield volcano

57. What is the Portuguese term for the equatorial rainforest of the Amazon basin?
Selva

58. The gradual soaking away of surface water into the soil is called what?
Seepage

59. What geological term describes conical hills formed, especially in the tundra, when water collected in underground pools trapped by permafrost gets pushed upward?
Pingos

60. The region of the Southern Hemisphere, between latitude 40 degrees south and 50 degrees south, where there are no barriers to an uninterrupted flow of the Westerlies, is known by what name?
Roaring Forties

61.   Which hemisphere has the summer solstice, the longest day of the
        year, on or near June 21st ?
        Northern Hemisphere

62.   MCSs are organized thunderstorm complexes that move across a
        region east of the Rockies, usually during the nighttime hours.
        What does the term "MCS" stand for?
        Mesoscale Convective System

63.   Name the scale that ranges from 1 to 17 that measures wind speed
        and effects associated with specific wind speeds. (Note: Forces 13
        to 17 apply to special cases. Taiwan and mainland China use them
        to measure tropical cyclones)
        Beaufort Scale

64.   The oxygen- and nutrient-rich Cromwell Current, a submarine
        river in the Galapagos, brings food supplies to the Galapagos
        penguins. What phenomenon brings these nutrients from the
        current to the surface?
        Upwelling

65.   A huge, dome-shaped intrusive body of igneous rock that extends
        towards the surface is known by what term?
        Batholith or pluton
        (Note: A pluton is a relatively small intrusive body. A batholith is
        much bigger and may contain many plutons. The Sierra Nevada
        Batholith of eastern California forms the largest mountain range
        in the continental United States. You may see an example of
        a pluton in Spirit Mountain, Nevada, where you can identify
        plutons as white granites poking through surrounding gray
        volcanic rocks.)

66.   What is the name of a violent, circular, swirling movement in the
        open sea where two tidal currents meet?
        Whirlpool

67. A prairie grassland landscape, with steep, sculptured rocks and buttes and minimal vegetation, found in places such as South Dakota, is known by what term?
Badland

68. The erosion of rock by moving ice can carve deep bowl-like basins known as cirques. What is the geological name for the narrow ridge that rises when two cirques form side by side?
Arête

69. When parallel cirques meet, they may cross the arête and form a pass. What is the name for this type of pass?
Col

70. Moorings on the ocean floor, which resemble barnacles, collect water pressure data to estimate wave heights. What are these moorings called—Barnys or Altimeters?
Barnys

71. What term describes the separation of a stream into two parts, which results in the creation of distributaries?
Bifurcation

72. What term describes the layer of water in which change of salinity is maximal—Halocline or Thermocline?
Halocline

73. The measurement of altitude is to altimetry as the study of underwater depth is to what?
Bathymetry

74. Marshes, swamps, and bogs could all be described as types of what biome?
Wetland biome

75. What term describes a small mountain lake that sometimes occupies a depression created by an alpine glacier?
Tarn

76. What term describes the circulation of water through lakes, rivers, groundwater, the ocean, and the atmosphere?
Hydrologic cycle (water cycle)

77. Meltwater from a glacier's surface often carves a nearly cylindrical, vertical shaft that extends through a glacier. What is the term for this shaft?
Moulin

78. A semi-permanent low-pressure area in what body of water that borders the Seward Peninsula and Kodiak Island is responsible for much of the storms that produce rain and snow on the west coast of the United States during the winter?
Gulf of Alaska

79. Which hemisphere has more land in the temperate zone?
Northern Hemisphere

80. A line on a map or chart that connects points of equal water depth is known by what term?
Isobath

81. What is the soil layer is made up of decomposed plant and animal matter?
Humus

82. Global warming has had a tremendous impact on the high mountains of the world. One of the impacts could be described by the term GLOF, which means the outburst of floods from what physical entity on these mountains?
Glacial lakes (GLOF—glacial lake outburst flood)

83. When cold air comes in contact with the highlands of a terrain and is cooled further, it becomes denser than the air at the same elevation but farther from the slope. Often a common feature in Antarctica, what is the term for the downslope winds that result?
Katabatic winds (drainage winds and glacier winds may be acceptable)

84. Named after the largest South African ethnic group, what is the term for the twenty-four hour time that is used throughout scientific and military communities and is related to UTC (Universal Time Coordinate) or GMT (Greenwich Mean Time)?
Zulu Time

85. What type of clouds appears in the sky as a flat uniform layer?
Stratus

86. Name the phenomenon where snow cover on the earth results in increased cooling.
Reflectivity of ice (Albedo)

87. A raised pathway across water or marshes is known by what name?
Causeway

88. The disruptive phenomenon where the earth cools following a mega-volcanic super eruption is known by what name?
Volcanic winter

89. As carbon dioxide increases, a fundamental property of ocean chemistry, measuring how acidic or alkaline the water is, varies. What is the chemical term for this property?
pH

90. The Keeling Curve is associated with measuring the variation in concentration of what gas in the atmosphere?
Carbon dioxide

91. The Sarma, Kultuk, and Barguzin are what kind of physical phenomena common in the Lake Baikal region?
Winds

92. Which of these choices does not belong and why: Methane, CO2, Water Vapor, and Neon.
Neon, because it is not a greenhouse gas

93. What is the name of the Mediterranean wind that comes from the Sahara and brings rain and fog to southern Europe?
Sirocco

94. What is the name of the type of rock that is formed from calcium carbonate of dead animals?
Sedimentary

95. Evergreen conifers that occur north of the temperate zone are characteristic of what type of biome?
Taiga

96. What is the name of the localized elevation that develops when a stream or ocean current deposits granular material, often constituting a hazard to navigation?
Sandbank (Sandbar and shoal are also acceptable)

97. The spiral pattern of winds flowing out of a high-pressure cell is known by what term?
Anticyclone

98. According to scientists, global warming could result in the rising of sea levels because of the expansion of seawater and the melting of what perennial cover formed over land?
Land ice (ice cover is also acceptable)

99. Temperate forests in the Northern Hemisphere are found in a region between which two latitudes?
Tropic of Cancer and the Arctic Circle

100. What part of a hurricane contains the strongest winds?
Eye wall

101. During World War II, the Japanese used a high-altitude flow of air to fly balloons at 30,000 feet across the Pacific to the United States. What is the name of this wind pattern?
Jet stream

102. What type of wind causes the aurora borealis?
Solar wind

103. According to scientists, melting sea ice in the Arctic may open up a sea route connecting the Atlantic and the Pacific oceans via waterways in the Canadian Arctic. Name the route sought by explorers for centuries as a possible trade route and first navigated by Roald Amundsen from 1903 to 1906.
Northwest Passage

104. The instability of superheated lava as it enters the ocean results in the formation of cracks and an ocean-facing scarp near its leading edge. Often seen on the southeast slope of the Kilauea Volcano in Hawaii, this area of seaward-facing cracks and scarps is known by what term?
Lava Bench

105. What is the term for the exceptionally high sea level that is reached during cyclonic conditions?
Storm surge

106. What is the type of tree found in temperate zones that drops its leaves in the fall?
Deciduous

107. As per the National Center for Atmospheric Research, Colorado, carbon dioxide cools Earth's atmosphere, which stretches from 60 miles to nearly 400 miles above the planet's surface. This region is known by what name?
Thermosphere

108. What term describes the remains of organisms that have been preserved for a very long time?
Fossil

109. The Thermohaline Conveyor Belt describes the circulation of ocean currents driven by the cooling and sinking of water masses in the North Atlantic, circulation of the ensuing cold water down through the Atlantic entering into the Pacific and the Indian oceans, and finally returning as warm upper currents in the south Atlantic. "Thermo" refers to the temperature of water. What does "haline" refer to?
Saltiness

110. The conical remains of an extinct volcano that lie below the ocean surface are known by what term?
Seamount

111. Some of the largest geological features on Earth consist of interconnected chains of mountains spread over the ocean floors of our planet. These features are known by what name?
Mid-ocean ridges

112. The flat-topped remains of an extinct volcano that break above the surface of water before subsiding are known by what geological term?
Guyot

113. Eucalyptus trees in Australia and the deciduous trees of the Sierra Nevadas are found in what type of forests—Boreal Forests or Temperate Evergreen Forests?
Temperate Evergreen Forests

114. In the zone of aeration, which lies just above the zone of temporary and permanent saturation, what fills the spaces between particles of soil and rock?
Air

115. Particles of material carried and deposited by water or wind are known by what term?
Sediment

116. What is the level at which one notices a marked change in the groundwater zone between the zone of aeration, where some pores are open, and the zone of saturation, where water fills the crevices in the rock?
Water table
(Note: "Water table" describes the upper surface of a groundwater zone)

117. Because the continental crust has a much lower density than the mantle, crustal blocks can be envisioned as floating on the mantle in the same way that icebergs float on seawater. This process is known by what geological term?
Isostasy
(Note: Mt. Everest is supported by the thick continental crust below it. This crust floats on the mantle. It is a balancing act.)

118.   Large, steep-sloped volcanoes like Mt. Fuji are built up of
        alternating layers of more viscous lava and pyroclastic deposits.
        What is the name given to this type of volcano?
        Stratovolcano

119.   When a magma chamber is emptied, the overlying rock loses
        support and the volcano's summit collapses. What physical feature
        results from this phenomenon?
        Caldera

120.   Name the item that does not belong in this group and explain
        why: herb, shrub, kelp, understory, canopy.
        Kelp, because it is underwater

121.   Scientific studies have suggested 80 percent of the ice and snow
        at the summit of Mt. Kilimanjaro has melted. This worldwide
        occurrence is attributed to what phenomenon?
        Global warming

122.   What do you call a fan-shaped mass of sediments deposited when
        streams flow from mountains to flat land?
        Alluvial fan

123.   When the action of waves is weak and that of a river is strong, an
        irregular-shaped delta, such as the Mississippi River Delta, is formed
        and extends out into a larger body of water. What is the term for this
        type of delta—a Bird's-foot delta or a classical Greek delta?
        Bird's foot delta

124.   When meltwater streams erode vertical sinkholes, tunnels, and
        chambers within the ice of glaciers, what structure is formed?
        Ice cave (meltwater caves is acceptable)

125. Successive fracturing of glacial ice by irregular sections of bedrock produces a series of parallel cracks in the ice. What is the glacial term for the high ice pinnacles that are formed when these cracks intersect?
Serac

126. Scientists extract long cylindrical columns of ice from places like Antarctica and examine how the ice changes with depth. Trapped air bubbles, the level of carbon dioxide, and pollution in the ice core all help determine what phenomenon in Earth's history?
Fluctuations in climate

127. Name the formation among the following that does not belong and explain why: star, linear, barchan, stalactite
Stalactite, because it is not associated with sand dunes

128. Put the following biomes in order of increasing precipitation. Taiga, Hot Deserts, Deciduous Forests, Tundra
Hot Deserts, Tundra, Taiga, Deciduous Forests

129. The Camargue, located within the Rhone Delta in France, consists of salt marshes, saltwater, lagoons, freshwater ponds, and dunes. This is an example of what type of ecosystem?
Wetland

130. Put the following eras in order from most ancient to most recent. Mesozoic, Precambrian, Cenozoic, Paleozoic
Precambrian, Paleozoic, Mesozoic, Cenozoic

131. Lakes with no outlets are formed when large blocks of melting ice become surrounded by debris from glaciers. This type of lake is known by what name?
Kettle lake

132. Cumulonimbus clouds have a distinctive anvil-shaped top near the boundary between the troposphere and the stratosphere. This boundary is known by what name?
      Tropopause

133. What term describes the coastal area between the highest high tide and the lowest low tide where organisms survive despite being pounded by the waves constantly—Continental shelf or Intertidal zone?
      Intertidal Zone

134. What do you call the global winds near 30 degrees north and south latitudes that result from earth's rotation, deflecting air from west to east as the air moves towards the polar regions—Westerlies or Polar easterlies?
      Westerlies

135. Generally, clouds that produce rain or snow are associated with a Latin term for "dark rain clouds". Name this term.
      Nimbus

CHAPTER 9

Cultural Geography

1. Other than language, what has been a defining component of cultural identity—religion or wealth?
Religion

2. What is the name for the clan-based culture of isolated populations— Popular Culture or Folk Culture?
Folk Culture

3. Large urban population lends itself to what type of culture—Pastoral Culture or Popular Culture?
Popular Culture

4. What term describes generalizations about other people's cultures based on your own cultural norms—Ethnocentrism or Xenocentrism?
Ethnocentrism

5. Ambohimanga, the ancient site of the Merina Kingdom, is a hub of spiritual pilgrimage near the capital city of an African island country. Name this capital city.
Antananarivo

6. Diwali, the national Hindu street festival, is a major event in what Caribbean island nation that has Chaguanas as its largest municipality and is home to the world's largest natural asphalt lake?
Trinidad and Tobago

7. The Antonini Musuem in Nasca is known for its collection of artifacts from the pre-Incan city of Cahuachi in what country?
Peru

8. The Kyaikhtiyo Pagoda is a huge boulder precariously resting on a cliff on a gorge in the Mon State of what Asian country?
Myanmar

9. Good Friday and Easter are important holidays for Christians in the town of Trapani in what Italian region?
Sicily

10. The town of Siret is well-known for its rich collection of old, carved Jewish tombstones. This town is located in the northeastern part of what European country?
Romania

11. The Menin Gate Memorial honors soldiers who died in Ypres Salient during World War I. This memorial is located in what European country?
Belgium

12. What language, other than Mandarin, Hindi, English, and Spanish, is considered to be among the top five widely spoken languages in the world?
Arabic

13. Name the world's single largest language family.
Indo-European

14. Dravidian is a language group mostly found in what country?
India

15. Romance language belongs to what language group—Indo-European or Austro-Asiatic?
Indo-European

16. The Daic language family spoken in many parts of Southeast Asia belongs to what major language family—Austronesian or Japanese-Korean?
Austronesian

17. What is the most practiced Islamic sect in Africa—Shia Muslim or Sunni Muslim?
Sunni Muslim

18. What was the world's only Hindu kingdom until 2006?
Nepal

19. Which is the dominant Christian denomination in Australia?
Protestant

20. Which is a monotheistic religion—Shintoism or Islam?
Islam

21. Which of these monuments in Jerusalem is more sacred to Judaism—Western Wall or Dome of the Rock?
Western Wall

22. Name the ancient Mexican city whose name means "City of the Gods."
Teotihuacan

23. Fugu is a traditional puffer fish that is a delicacy in what country that owns the Pacific island of Marcus?
Japan

24. Wat is a traditional food in what African country on the Horn of Africa that has Jima as an important mining town in its highlands region?
Ethiopia

25. Sauerkraut is an appetizing sour cabbage dish that originated in Western Europe's most populous country. Name this country.
Germany

26. The Chartres Cathedral, Amiens and Reims are among the finest examples of Gothic architecture in what country?
France

27. The megalith of Carnac lies on the southwest coast of what cultural and administrative French region on the Gulf of Morbihan?
Brittany

28. The *Kumbh Mela* (Pitcher Festival) occurs every three years in one of the four holy cities in what Asian country?
India

29. The Topkapi Palace, known for its collection of relics of the Prophet Mohammad, is in what city in Turkey?
Istanbul

30. What site in the heart of Old Jerusalem is held sacred by Jews, Christians, and Muslims?
The Temple Mount

31. Lumbini, the birthplace of the Buddha, is a pilgrimage center in what Asian country?
Nepal

32. The Jallabia is a long, wide dress worn by men in Islamic countries including what country that has Tanta as its largest city in its delta region?
Egypt

33. Baklava, a dessert made of pastry, is very popular in a secular, constitutional republic established in 1923 on the Eastern Mediterranean. Name this country.
Turkey

34. Skansen is the world's first open air museum in the largest city in the Nordic region. Name this city that is nicknamed the "water city" and is made up of fourteen islands.
Stockholm

35. Millet and a porridge made from a tall, syrup-yielding tropical grass grown for its sweet juice are the primary sources of nourishment in Botswana. Name this grass.
Sorghum

36. Pavlova is a dessert made of meringue and cream and is usually topped with kiwifruit. This is a popular dish in which country that was discovered in 750 AD by the Polynesian explorer Kupe?
New Zealand

37. The Butanding Festival that coincides with the arrival of whale sharks in its coastal regions attracts many tourists to Bicol in what Asian country that is well-known for its Banaue Rice Terraces?
Philippines

38. What do you call a simplified language used mainly for communicating between different cultures—Pidgin or Lingua Franca?
Pidgin

39. When Pidgin becomes common enough to become the primary language it is called a Creole. Name the Creole that evolved from the Arabic and Bantu languages in eastern Africa.
Swahili

40. When existing languages are adopted by members of different cultures, what alternative to Pidgin and Creole is formed?
Lingua Franca

41. Toponymy reveals the history of a region and the values of the people. Toponymy is the study of what—place-names or language origins?
Place-Names

42. Bo trees are sacred to what religion?
Buddhism

43. Varanasi, India is to Hinduism as Ise, Japan is to what?
Shintoism

44. Ganges River is to Hinduism as Jordan River is to what?
Christianity

45. Voodoo melds beliefs from African and Caribbean local religions with beliefs from Christianity. What do you call this type of religion—Polytheistic or Syncretic?
Syncretic Religion

46. The Sistine Chapel is in what European country?
Vatican City

47. The Arena Chapel is located in Padua in what European country?
Italy

48. The largest Matsu Festival is celebrated in Meizhou Island in what southeastern Chinese province also known for its well-known cuisine?
Fujian

49. If one visits Alsace and Lorraine, located in northeast France, they would likely find food that has a strong culinary influence from what country?
Germany

50. Clothing from Europe's sole Muslim-majority nation tends
     to express Turkish influences as a result of about 500 years of
     Ottoman Rule. Name this country.
     Albania

51. Costumes from a Balkan country reflect their independence from
     Yugoslavia and also have Greek, Albanian, and Turkish elements
     alongside their native Slavic heritage because of its geography.
     Name this country.
     Macedonia

52. Toga was the standard dress in what ancient European culture?
     Roman

53. Lederhosen, meaning "leather trousers", is a type of clothing worn
     by people in the alpine regions of what country?
     Germany

54. What term often associated with well-known European
     architecture refers to the period immediately following the
     Romanesque period and preceding the Renaissance?
     Gothic

55. Sushi is to Japan as Eggplant Parmigiana is to what?
     Italy

56. Sish Kebab is to Persia as Hummus is to what?
     Middle East

57. The festival of Gion Matsuri is to Japan as Purim is to what?
     Israel

58. Cinco de Mayo is to Mexico as Jamhuri is to what?
     Kenya

59. Name the official language spoken in the provinces of the Netherlands besides Dutch?

Frisian

60. The Beret is the traditional hat of Basque shepherds and is worn by many men in what European country?

France

61. The Yanomami Indians live in the Amazonian rainforests of Brazil and what other country?

Venezuela

62. Glastonbury has been a religious center since pre-Christian times. This is in what political unit of the United Kingdom?

England

63. About 5,000 years ago, the Beaker people built the impressive earth mound called "Newgrange" in the Boyne Valley of what European country?

Ireland

64. The 12th century statue of La Moreneta, which means "Black Madonna" is the highlight of Montserrat, a sacred Christian site in the Pyrenees Mountains of what country on the Iberian Peninsula?

Spain

65. In 1500 B.C.E., which civilization constructed their capital city of La Venta on an island where the Rio Tonala River runs into the Gulf of Mexico?

Olmec

66. What ancient Mexican city, located on the Yucatan Peninsula, is filled with the images of the serpent god Quetzalcoatl?

Chichen Itza

67. The city of Hampi is a sacred site in the state of Karnataka in
     what country?
     India

68. The Abatao Cultural Tour provides an insight into the traditional
     cultural practices of what country that has 33 coral islands divided
     among three island groups: the Gilbert Islands, the Phoenix
     Islands, and the Line Islands?
     Kiribati

69. Borobudur, the world-famous stupa complex of shrines dedicated
     to Buddha was erected by the Shailendra Dynasty in the
     eighteenth century C.E. and is located in what Asian country?
     Indonesia

70. Koya-san is a major center of Japanese Buddhism in the northern
     Wakayama prefecture, located in the Kii mountain range on what
     Japanese island?
     Honshu Island

71. The Greek Orthodox Monastery of Saint Catherine in Egypt is at
     the foot of what sacred mountain in the Middle East?
     Mount Sinai

72. Bahir Dar is home to the traditional papyrus reed boats called
     tankwas. These are made by the Woyto people, who live on the
     shores of what lake on the Horn of Africa?
     Lake Tana

73. The Late Bronze Age exhibit of the famed Uluburun shipwreck,
     discovered near the city of Ka in the province of Antalya, made
     the Bodrum Musuem of Underwater Archaeology a major
     attraction in what country?
     Turkey

74. Colossal statues of Ramses II are seated at the main entrance to the "Great Temple." Name the UNESCO World Heritage site where this is located.
Abu Simbel

75. The well-known Ceramics Museum is located in the Asian city of Zibo, which is considered to be the birthplace of Cuju, an ancient game of football. Zibo is located in what country?
China

76. In 1846, Georg Ramsauer discovered the Celtic settlement in Halstatt in what country that shares the Bavarian Alps with Germany?
Austria

77. The 'Caves of the Thousand Buddhas' are situated at Mogao, south-east of the oasis town of Dunhuang, in what province that has Lanzhou as its provincial capital?
Gansu

78. What peak situated at the intersection of three mountain ranges (the Sierra Nevada, the Cascades and the Klamath Mountains) was sacred to the Modoc Native American tribes?
Mount Shasta

79. The island monastery of Mont Saint Michel is a well-known site on what French coast near its juncture with the peninsula of Brittany?
Normandy

80. Name the Aegean seaport in Turkey's Izmir Province that is home to the Temple of Artemis and was a pilgrimage city to both the Greeks and the Romans.
Ephesus

81. The Tarxien, constructed between 3600 and 2500 BC, is part of the seven megalithic temples that are classified under the UNESCO World Heritage sites listing. This is located in what island country about 60 miles from Sicily?
Malta

82. The most sacred shrine of the Sikh religion is in what Indian city?
Amritsar

83. Baalbek is an ancient Roman city in the northeastern part of what Arab country whose Christian population identify themselves as descendants of the ancient Canaanites?
Lebanon

84. Segovia, a UNESCO World Heritage site, is in what Spanish region?
Castile-Leon

85. The National War Memorial of Canada is in the center of Confederation Square in what city?
Ottawa

86. The Great Mosque of Samarra is in what Arab country?
Iraq

87. The Tapati Festival is an important event in what Polynesian island in the southeastern Pacific Ocean belonging to Chile?
Easter Island

88. Jantar Mantar, the world's largest stone observatory has the world's largest sundial that is 90 feet tall. This is in Jaipur, in the state of Rajasthan, in what Asian country?
India

89. What broader term describes the social relationships between people who are related by blood, marriage and other human binding ritual—Kinship or Camaraderie?
Kinship

90. Mandarin Chinese is the most widely spoken first language in the world. Which of these languages is more widely spoken—Bengali or Russian?
Bengali

91. In the 6th century C.E., Zen Buddhism originated in what country?
China

92. Name the well-known ancient North African city of Phoenician origin that clashed with Rome in the Punic Wars?
Carthage

93. The early Middle Ages have been called the Dark Ages because—(a) very few innovations took place during that period or (b) there were very few written records to illuminate what happened during that period?
(b) There were very few written records to illuminate what happened during that period

94. In 1519, Hernan Cortes reached what Aztec capital?
Tenochtitlan

95. Mexico City stands at the site of what ancient city—Tenochtitlan or Teotihuacan?
Tenochtitlan

96. The Incan king Pachacuti is credited with the building of what magnificent retreat in the Andes?
Machu Picchu

97.   A fairy-tale ballet, composed in 1892 by Peter Ilyich Tchaikovsky, is one of the most popular Russian ballets and is generally performed during the Christmas season in the United States. Name this ballet.
The Nutcracker

98.   Hagiographa is a term for "sacred writing" in what European language?
Greek

99.   Once a tiny fishing port, an English city on the estuary of the Mersey River was named the 2008 European Capital of Culture, marking the 800th anniversary of King John's signing of the city's charter in August 1207. Name the city.
Liverpool

100.   A country formed from a mixture of cultural groups with different languages and unified by an official language is known as—a polyglot state or a theocratic state?
Polyglot state

101.   In 1984, archaeologists discovered a longboat from about 300 B.C.E. that had sailed the Humber River, a North Sea inlet on the east coast of England. This was considered to be one of the trademarks of what culture known for their farms and hill-forts?
Celtic

102.   Belarusan, Sorbian, and Serbian belong to what language group?
Slavic

103.   Which country has a larger Muslim population—Bangladesh or Pakistan?
Pakistan

104. According to Maori legend, what peak is considered to be a frozen Maori warrior?

     Mount Cook

105. Talmud written in the Aramaic language is one of the most important texts in what religion?

     Judaism

CHAPTER 10

Current Affairs

1. In October 2010, toxic sludge along the Danube River devastated the village of Kolontar in what country bordering Croatia along the River Drava?
Hungary

2. In September 2010, remnants of the tropical storm Matthew drenched the city of Villahermosa in what Latin American country?
Mexico

3. In September 2010, the Basque separatist group ETA (Euskadi Ta Askatasuna) declared that they were willing to accept a permanent cease-fire in what country?
Spain

4. In October 2010, an accident threatened the life of two American balloonists near Bari in what European country?
Italy

5. In October 2010, a police revolt paralyzed what country that has Cayambe as one of its highest volcanoes?
Ecuador

6. In October 2010, Prime Minister Valdis Dombrovskis won the general election in which country that has Liepaja (pronounced LEE-eh-PAH-yah), the city where "wind was born", as one of its largest on the Baltic Sea coast?
Latvia

7. In October 2010, the ancient pagan tradition of Druidry was accepted as a religion under charity law in what country whose claims on the North Atlantic islet of Rockall are disputed by Ireland, Denmark, and Iceland?
United Kingdom

8. In October 2010, 33 miners from Copiapo were rejoined with their families after weeks of being trapped in a copper and gold mine. Copiapo is in what country that owns Wellington Island?
Chile

9. In October 2010, a Hebrew daily newspaper revealed the construction of 54 new housing units in Ariel in what Palestinian region?
West Bank

10. In October 2010, the exhibit "Michelangelo: The Drawings of a Genius" featuring 120 drawings were on display in the Albertina Museum in the capital city of a European country bordering Slovakia and Switzerland. Name this country.
Austria

11. In October 2010, more than 200 passengers were evacuated from a ferry burning on the Baltic Sea near Cuxhaven in what country south of Denmark?
Germany

12. In October 2010, the New York Times reported that an Asian country that is the exclusive house of rare-earth deposits has halted shipments of these elements to the United States. Name this country that shares the Gulf of Tonkin with Vietnam.
China

13. In October 2010, Mount Merapi, whose name translates as "Fire Mountain," erupted, affecting thousands of people in the world's largest archipelago. Name this country.
Indonesia

14. In December 2010, a West African nation that has the largest manmade lake in the world was set to pump its first commercial oil after the discovery of the offshore Jubilee Field three years ago. Name this nation.
Ghana

15. October 2010 marked the 10,000ᵗʰ birthday of one of the oldest continually inhabited settlements on the West Bank near the Jordan River. Name this city.
Jericho

16. In October 2010, the world's longest tramway, spanning 3.5 miles across the Vorotan River gorge, opened. Name this country that shares the Vorotan River basin with Azerbaijan.
Armenia

17. In October 2010, a dispute flared between Japan and another country over a group of islands that Japan calls the Senkaku Islands. Name the other country, who calls this island group the Diaoyu Islands.
China

18. In November 2010, Hurricane Thomas threatened Kingstown, the chief port of which Caribbean country?
St. Vincent and Grenadines

19. On January 1, 2011, which country became the first former Soviet state to adopt the Euro when it switched from its former currency, the kroon?
Estonia

20. In November 2010, there was an airline disaster in a Caribbean country that has the historic center of Camagüey, a UNESCO World Heritage site. Name this country.
Cuba

21. In November 2010, authorities expressed hope that Hungary's massive red sludge would not pollute Europe's second longest river. Name this river.
Danube River

22. In November 2010, environmentalists blocked a train carrying nuclear waste to Germany from near the city of Caen in which European country?
France

23. In November 2010, the world's largest statue of Jesus Christ was about to be installed in Swiebodzin in what European country on the Gulf of Gdansk?
Poland

24. In October 2010, which military-ruled Asian country bordering India hoisted a new flag in replacement of the older flag with a red background and a blue patch on the top left corner with corn in it?
Myanmar

25. In October 2010, typhoon Megi became the strongest typhoon in what body of water off of Asia's coast that contains Brunei's oil and natural gas reserves?
South China Sea

26. In November 2010, Lynda Lovejoy unsuccessfully campaigned to become the first woman President of the largest Indian Reservation in the United States. Name this reservation.
Navajo Reservation

27. In October 2010, the 35-mile Gotthard Base Tunnel was set to become the world's longest rail tunnel when a European country connected its German speaking region with its Italian speaking region. Name this non-European Union country.
Switzerland

28.   In October 2010, which landlocked country signed a pact with
      Peru that allowed it some rights to run its naval vessels from a
      tiny dock on the Pacific?
      Bolivia

29.   In November 2010, the northernmost mosque in North America
      opened in the town of Inuvik, north of the Arctic Circle. This is
      in what Canadian administrative region?
      Northwest Territories

30.   In November 2010, the world's largest cocoa producer, with the
      Komoe as one of its most important rivers, held its first election
      after a decade of unrest. Name this country.
      Cote d'Ivoire

31.   In October 2010, a tornado killed several people in the town of
      Pozo del Tigre in the second largest country in the MERCOSUR
      Latin America Trade Organization by area. Name this country.
      Argentina

32.   In November 2010, heavy flooding resulted in loss of property
      in the town of Hat Yai in the Songkhla province of what Asian
      country bordering Cambodia and Myanmar?
      Thailand

33.   In November 2010, an earthquake rocked the town of Kraljevo, a
      town that is sometimes nicknamed the "City of the Kings". Name
      the country, located on the Balkan Peninsula, in which this occurred.
      Serbia

34.   In November 2010, Russian President Dmitry Medvedev visited
      one of the islands in what mineral-rich island group that was
      seized from Japan at the end of World War II?
      Kuril Islands

35. In November 2010, clashes erupted between the government and Karen rebels in Myawaddy and near the Three Pagoda Pass in the Tenasserim Mountain Range, which is located on the border of Myanmar and what other country?
Thailand

36. In November 2010, Tanzanian President Jakaya Kikwete announced a proposal to build a controversial national highway through what national park that is home to the "Great Migration" of wildlife?
Serengeti National Park

37. In October 2010, the island of St. Maarten celebrated greater autonomy following the breakup of the Netherlands Antilles. Name its capital city in which the festivities took place.
Philipsburg

38. In November 2010, a public square in a European city was renamed "Nov. 9, 1989 Square" in honor of the collapse of what wall 21 years ago?
Berlin Wall

39. In October 2010, a 650-foot ferry that exploded was finally brought under control near the island of Langland between the Bay of Kiel and the Great Belt in what European country?
Denmark

40. In November 2010, Google Inc. inadvertently became involved in a controversy when its mapping services attributed the disputed islet of Perejil (Parsley) first to Spain and then to what African country that sometimes calls it "Leila?"
Morocco

41.   In November 2010, there was a major mining explosion in
       Atarau, site of the largest-known coking coal deposits near the
       Paparoa Ranges in which country?
       New Zealand

42.   In November 2010, which country completed the world's largest
       census, requiring 6 million census takers to complete the task?
       China

43.   In November 2010, the Organization of American States leader
       urged Nicaragua and a Central American country to withdraw
       security forces from a tense border zone. Name this country whose
       entire length is covered by Guanacaste Mountain Range, Central
       Mountain Range, and Talamanca Mountain Ranges.
       Costa Rica

44.   In November 2010, there was a major polio outbreak in one of
       sub-Saharan Africa's main oil producing regions that used to be
       the French region of Middle Congo before its independence in
       1960. Name this country.
       Republic of the Congo

45.   In November 2010, EU Council President Herman Van Rompuy
       delivered his State of Europe speech at the Pergamon Museum in
       which capital city?
       Berlin

46.   In September 2010, Red Cross officials from North and South
       Korea failed to reach an agreement about restarting reunions
       between families separated by the Korean War when they met at
       the border town of Kaesong in which country?
       North Korea

47. In October 2010, the Shiite Opposition became the largest bloc in the parliament of which Arab kingdom that was once known to Greeks as Tylos and is traditionally well-known for its shipping industry?
Bahrain

48. In November 2010, Yale University agreed to return thousands of artifacts taken by scholar Hiram Bingham III between 1911 and 1915 from what ancient site in South America?
Machu Picchu

49. In 2010, scientists released genetically modified mosquitoes in an experiment to fight dengue fever in a British Overseas Territory that consists of three main islands and is located about 480 miles south of Miami. Name this territory.
Cayman Islands

50. In November 2010, Pacific Rim leaders tried to smooth divisions over currency policies in a forum held in Yokohama in what country?
Japan

51. In November 2010, a smoking ban was met with anger by citizens in a Balkan country whose caves and potholes are classified as speleological natural monuments. Name this country that has the Stopića Pećina caves as one of its major attractions.
Serbia

52. According to reports in 2010, the underwater methane that poses a risk to millions of people living around a lake could also be used to generate power for its bordering countries. Name this lake shared by Rwanda and the Democratic Republic of the Congo.
Lake Kivu

53. In September 2010, Hurricane Earl threatened the town of Nags Head in which U.S. state?
North Carolina

54. In September 2010, Typhoon Kompasu became the strongest storm to hit what Asian peninsula that is known for its "demilitarized zone," a temporary geopolitical boundary created to end hostilities in 1953?
Korean Peninsula

55. In August 2010, tensions were unusually high during the customary parades by Protestant groups emphasizing their loyalty to the British Crown, which often create friction with their Roman Catholic neighbors. Name this political unit of the United Kingdom.
Northern Ireland

56. In August 2010, the centennial of the birth of the Catholic Church's beatified nun was celebrated in Ahmedabad, Gujarat in what Asian country?
India

57. In October 2010, elections were held in the heart-shaped country ethnically split between Serbs, Bosniaks, and Croats. Name this country bordering Croatia.
Bosnia and Herzegovina

58. In October 2010, the first elections in 20 years were held in which country that has Nay Pyi Taw as its capital city?
Myanmar (Burma)

59. In November 2010, a South American country bordering Brazil, Bolivia, and Argentina denied authorization for a British-led scientific expedition for fear of introducing new European diseases to its indigenous people. Name this country.
Paraguay

60. In November 2010, an outbreak of the parasitic tropical disease Kala Azar killed more than 300 people in the most populous country in North Africa. Name this country.
Egypt

61. In November 2010, authorities were concerned about the outbreak of dengue fever in a South American country that has Pico da Neblina as its highest peak near its border with Venezuela. Name this country.
Brazil

62. In November 2010, North Korea bombed the tiny South Korean island of Yeonpyeong just south of the disputed maritime border in what sea?
Yellow Sea

63. In August 2010, lawmakers in Catalonia outlawed bullfighting making it the first region to ban this tradition in what country?
Spain

64. In August 2010, First Lady Michelle Obama met the king and queen of what country during a luncheon on the Mediterranean resort island of Mallorca?
Spain

65. In August 2010, which large country that owns the treeless Commander Islands, which are geologically related to the Aleutian Islands, announced a ban on grain exports through the end of 2010 in response to a scorching drought in that country?
Russia

66. In August 2010, in response to the sinking of the Cheonan warship in a March 2010 torpedo attack by its rival, which Asian country conducted a military drill and dropped sonar buoys into the Yellow Sea?
South Korea

67. In September 2010, a section of a gas pipeline exploded in San Bruno, a suburb of what city in northern California?
San Francisco

68. In September 2010, a devastating earthquake rocked a region near what city just south of Porirua, New Zealand?
Wellington

69. In September 2010, President Alvaro Colom visited landslide ravaged regions in what country that has Quetzaltenango as one of its major cities?
Guatemala

70. July 9, 2011 marked the independence of what country that has the city of Juba, on the Mountain Nile, as its capital?
South Sudan

71. In August-September 2010, the rising Bago River submerged low-lying regions in the town of Bago, formerly Pegu, which is located about 50 miles north of which Burmese city?
Yangon

72. In September 2010, government troops clashed with Abu Sayyaf rebels in a country whose Chocolate Hills in Bohol are a major tourist attraction. Name this country.
Philippines

73. In September 2010, elections were held in a Scandinavian country that has Finnish as its biggest immigrant group and has the beautiful town of Örebro by Lake Hjälmaren. Name this country.
Sweden

74. In September 2010, Hurricane Igor headed towards Hamilton, the capital of which overseas British Territory?
Bermuda

75. In September 2010, the Mai Mai militia was suspected of violence in what country that borders Lake Albert and Lake Mweru?
Democratic Republic of the Congo

76. In September 2010, Checkpoint Bravo was sold at auction for $58,000. This property was once used as the main autobahn checkpoint between East Germany and which city and Land (State) of the Federal Republic of Germany (West Germany) that was not constitutionally part of West Germany?
West Berlin

77. In July 2010, the ninth International Alphorn Festival was held in Nendaz in what European country whose Illgraben-Bhutan Bridge helps tourists appreciate the canyons of the picturesque Valais region?
Switzerland

78. In August 2010, an underground tomb housing an ancient marble coffin was discovered in what European capital that was formerly known as Angora?
Ankara

79. In August 2010, a Boeing 737 jetliner crashed in a thunderstorm on the Caribbean island of San Andres, about 80 miles from Nicaragua. This island is a property of what Latin American country?
Colombia

80. In August 2010, the opening of a new movie theater was an event for celebration for Palestinians in the city of Jenin, the third largest city in which Palestinian territory?
West Bank

81. In August 2010, the surging Indus River forced evacuation of several people in the historic town of Thatta in Pakistan's southernmost province. Name this province.
Sindh

82.   In July 2010, the nonpartisan Population Reference Bureau
       reported that with 267 people being born every minute and 108
       dying, the world's population will reach how many billion in
       2011 and more than 9 billion in 2050?
       7 billion

83.   In August 2010, a festival that takes its name from the famous
       1969 music festival on a farm near a town in the state of New
       York was held in Kostrzyn in Poland. Name this festival.
       The Woodstock Musical Festival

84.   In August 2010, there were concerns about a biological disaster
       following an oil spill that threatened the region where the
       Kalamazoo River reaches what Great Lake in United States?
       Lake Michigan

85.   In July 2010, Syrian President Bashar Assad met his bitter rival
       King Abdullah over concerns in Lebanon. King Abdullah is the
       ruler of the world's second largest crude oil producer after Russia.
       Name this nation.
       Saudi Arabia

86.   In August 2010, what kingdom that has the House of Orange as
       its royal family became the first NATO member to end its mission
       in Afghanistan. Name this country.
       Netherlands

87.   In August 2010, the most populous British Commonwealth
       country announced plans to import cheetahs from Africa and
       introduce them into their grasslands. Name this country.
       India

88. In August 2010, Stonehenge II, a replica of the original Stonehenge monument, was being moved from the town of Hunt to a site near Point Theater in Ingram. This move has been supported by the Hills Country Art Foundation in which southwestern U.S. state?
Texas

89. In September 2010, a bronze statue credited to the Sumerians was returned to the Iraqi National Museum. Sumerians were the inhabitants of what historical region in 5,000 B.C.E.?
Mesopotamia

90. In September 2010, at least 50 people were arrested during a pro-democracy protest in which African kingdom that has Lilangeni as its currency and Emlembe as its highest point?
Swaziland

91. In September 2010, President Goodluck Jonathan announced that he will contest in the presidential election in what OPEC country in Western Africa?
Nigeria

92. In October 2010, Néstor Kirchner, former President of a Latin American country died at his home in El Calafate, Santa Cruz Province, the second-largest and the least densely populated province in which country?
Argentina

93. In October 2010, an African country that has Mwanza as its major port on Lake Victoria, went to polls. Name this country.
Tanzania

94. In October 2010, Dilma Rousseff was elected as the first female President of South America's largest country. Name this country.
Brazil

95. In October 2010, the Emir of a peninsular country within the Arabian Peninsula bordering Saudi Arabia and the Persian Gulf was on a state visit to the United Kingdom. Name this country.
Qatar

96. In September 2010, a gas explosion killed many people in the city of Mashhad in what Asian country?
Iran

97. In October 2010, a Ghana-born doctor named Peter Bossman became the first black mayor of the city Piran in the southwestern part of what European country?
Slovenia

98. In October 2010, the United Arab Emirates closed its airspace to Defense Minister Peter MacKay from the largest Commonwealth nation over a growing dispute about aviation rights. Name this British Commonwealth.
Canada

99. In September 2010, a 1550 B.C.E. find of a teen dubbed "The Boy with the Amber Necklace" was displayed as evidence of the diversity of people who visited what ancient ring in Britain?
Stonehenge

100. According to reports in August 2010, a Vincent van Gogh painting was stolen from the Mahmoud Khalil Museum in the most populated Arab city in Africa. Name this city.
Cairo

BIBLIOGRAPHY

Barber, Nicola, Jason Hook, Patricia Levy, Chris Oxlade, and Sean Sheehan. *Question and Answer Encyclopedia: The USA.* New York: Parragon Publishing, 2005.

Britannica Online Encyclopedia. http://www.britannica.com/ [December 27, 2010].

British Broadcasting Corporation. http://www.bbc.co.uk/ [January 4, 2011]

CIA: The World Factbook. https://www/cia.gov/library/publications/the-world-factbook/ [December 27, 2010].

Claybourne, Anna, Gillian Doherty, and Rebecca Treays. *The Usborne Encyclopedia of Planet Earth.* New York: Scholastic, 2000.

Encyclopedia of Earth. http://www.eoearth.org/ [December 27, 2010].

Fuller, Barbara. *Germany.* Cultures of the World. Tarrytown, NY: Marshall Cavendish, 2004.

Ganeri, Anita, Hazel Mary Martell, and Brian Williams. *Encyclopedia of World History.* New York: Parragon Publishing, 2005.

Gofen, Ethel Caro. *France.* Cultures of the World. Tarrytown, NY: Marshall Cavendish, 1999.

Gray, Susan Heinrichs. First Reports book series. Bloomington, MN: Capstone Publishers, Compass Point Books, 2000–2002.

Green, Jen. *Ancient Celts.* Washington, DC: National Geographic Society, 2008.

Kansas City Star Newspapers. Kansas City, various dates.

Lye, Keith. *The New Children's Illustrated Atlas of the World.* Philadelphia: Running Press, Courage Books, 1999.

McNair, Sylvia. *U.S. Territories.* America the Beautiful Second Series. New York: Children's Press, 2001.

Miller, Millie, and Cyndi Nelson. *The United States of America: A State-by-State Guide.* New York: Scholastic, 1999.

National Estuarine Research Reserve System, http://www.nerrs.noaa.gov [December 27, 2010].

National Geographic Society. *The National Geographic Desk Reference.* Washington, DC: National Geographic Society, 1999.

National Geographic Society. *The National Geographic Kids Almanac.* Washington, DC: National Geographic Society, 2010.

National Geographic Society. *National Geographic Student Atlas of the World.* Updated ed. Washington, DC: National Geographic Society, 2004.

National Geographic Society. *National Geographic Student Atlas of the World.* Rev. ed. Washington, DC: National Geographic Society, 2005.

National Geographic Society. *National Geographic United States Atlas for Young Explorers.* Updated ed. Washington, DC: National Geographic Society, 2004.

National Geographic Society. *National Geographic World Atlas for Young Explorers.* Rev. ed. Washington, DC: National Geographic Society, 2003.

National Geographic Society. *National Geographic United States Atlas for Young Explorers.* Third Edition. Washington, DC: National Geographic Society, 2008.

National Geographic Society. *National Geographic World Atlas for Young Explorers.* Third Edition. Washington, DC: National Geographic Society, 2008.

National Geographic Society. *Sacred Places of a Lifetime.* Third Edition. Washington, DC: National Geographic Society, 2008.

National Park Service. http://www.nps.gov/olym/naturescience/forests. htm [December 27, 2010].

Olsen, Brad. *Sacred Places: 101 Spiritual Sites Around the World.* First Edition, San Francisco: CCC Publishing, 2000.

Oman, Anne H. *Weather: Nature in Motion.* Washington, DC: National Geographic Society, 2005.

Padilla, Michael J., Ioannis Miaoulis, and Martha Cyr. *Science Explorer: Earth Science.* Upper Saddle River, NJ: Pearson Prentice Hall, 2001.

Rajendra, Vijeya. *Iran.* Cultures of the World. Tarrytown, NY: Marshall Cavendish, 2004.

Rajendra, Vijeya, and Sundran Rajendra. *Australia.* Cultures of the World. Tarrytown, NY: Marshall Cavendish, Benchmark Books, 2002.

Ricciuti, Edward. *Chaparral.* Tarrytown, NY: Marshall Cavendish, Benchmark Books, 1996.

Sayre, April Pulley. *Taiga.* Exploring Earth's Biomes. Minneapolis: Lerner Publications, Twenty-First Century Books, 1994.

Sayre, April Pulley. *Temperate Deciduous Forest.* Exploring Earth's Biomes. Minneapolis: Lerner Publications, Twenty-First Century Books, 1994.

Sayre, April Pulley. *Tropical Rain Forest.* Exploring Earth's Biomes. Minneapolis: Lerner Publications, Twenty-First Century Books, 1994.

Sayre, April Pulley. *Tundra.* Exploring Earth's Biomes. Minneapolis: Lerner Publications, Twenty-First Century Books, 2000–2009.

Sheehan, Sean. *Austria.* Cultures of the World. Tarrytown, NY: Marshall Cavendish, 2003.

Smelt, Roselynn. *New Zealand.* Cultures of the World. Tarrytown, NY: Marshall Cavendish, 1998.

Smithsonian Institution. *Earth.* 1st Am. ed. New York: Smithsonian Institution, DK Publishing, 2003.

Steele, Philip. *The Kingfisher Young People's Atlas of the World.* New York: Kingfisher, 1997.

UNESCO World Heritage Centre. http://whc.unesco.org/ December 27, 2010].

U.S. Department of State. http://www.state.gov/ [January 4, 2011]

Webster's Online Dictionary. http://www.websters-dictionary-online.com

Whittow, John B. *The Penguin Dictionary of Physical Geography.* 2nd ed. New York: Penguin Books, 2000.

Wikipedia: The Free Encyclopedia. http://www.wikipedia.org/. Accessed May 2007–Nov 2011.

Wilkinson, Philip. *The Kingfisher Student Atlas.* Boston: Kingfisher, 2003.

Williams, Barbara. *World War II: Pacific.* Minneapolis: Lerner Publications, 2005.

Book Reviews

"The questions within this book are rigorous and require a dedicated student to spend many hours preparing for stiff competition. Iyer's personal experience with his sons' forays in the Geography Bee will certainly pay off for anyone who studies from this book. Although, for obvious ethical reasons, none of the questions are directly from previous Geography Bee competitions, Ram Iyer knows enough about the competition to lay out a solid ground plan. Another nice feature about this book is the fact that it is not some antediluvian text with archaic facts and numbers. It focuses on recent events that are relevant and will continue to play an important role in our rapidly changing global landscape. Iyer's book contains 10 sections focusing on the various continents of the world as well as one on current affairs and another on physical geography. There are dozens of questions within each section testing knowledge of rivers, mountains, lakes, etc."

By <u>Sebastian Albu</u> in <u>All News</u>, <u>Book Reviews</u>, <u>Education News</u>

Blogger News Network

<u>http://www.bloggernews.net/114853</u> (For a complete review)

From Geography Bee Contestants

"This book was so helpful! My dad/coach quizzed me with it and it really helped me prepare for the National Competition of the Geography Bee because I could kind of expect what type of questions they would ask. I loved the feeling of getting Ram's questions right! It gave me confidence."

—Isabella Contolini – The 2010 Colorado State Champion

Ram Iyer's *Geography Bee Demystified* contains information that will not only prepare one to compete successfully at the National Geographic Bee, but to also extend anyone's knowledge of our ever changing world.

—Arjun Venkataraman – The 2010 Ohio State Second Place Winner

Mr. Iyer's book was extremely helpful in preparing for the State as well as National competitions. If you are want to go farther and farther, this book will make all the difference. We've all heard of how tiebreakers can make or break the amount of success you have, this book gives you those types of questions. More importantly the questions put you through the thought process needed for answering those tough questions. It is well researched and packed with questions that will take you to the next level. This book should definitely be on everyone's wish list for this Christmas!

—Arjun Kandaswamy
(The 2009 National Geographic Bee Second Place Winner)

"Geography Bee Demystified is a good book for kids preparing for the bee with challenging quizzes."

—Zaroug Jaleel
(The 2009 Massachusetts Champion and the 2009 Top-Ten Finalist)

"Geography Bee Demystified is the invaluable foundation for anyone serious about the Geography Bee."

—Omkar Shende – The 2009 Michigan State Second Place Winner

"This is a great resource that helped me prepare for the National Geography Bee after winning the New Hampshire State Geography Bee. It is well organized and I would recommend it to anyone that wants to do well in the geography bee or just to strengthen their knowledge of world geography in this era of increasing globalization."

—Milan Sandhu
(The 2007 and 2008 New Hampshire State Champion and the 2008 Top-Ten Finalist)

The book was immensely useful for me to prepare for the National Geography Bee as it will be for the contestants to come.

"The *Geography Bee Demystified* is an excellent resource - a must read - for all those preparing for the National Geography Bee. Its comprehensive coverage allows one not only to prepare for the competition, but also to apply the knowledge gained for use in future studies in Geography, World Cultures and Earth Sciences.

The difficulty level of the questions in the book is especially appropriate for the questions in the National tournament, which are definitely harder than those in the State tournament. Going through the questions in the book helped me to properly gauge my preparedness level for the National competition. I count the book as one of the key study aids for my preparation."

—Nikhil Desai
(The 2008 California State Champion and the 2008 Top-Ten finalist at the Nationals)

ABOUT THE AUTHOR

Ram Iyer is a software engineer working in the Kansas City area. Although he has spent most of his career in the engineering field, his interests extend into the physical sciences, earth sciences, geography, history, world cultures, sports, and political science. He has traveled to many interesting places around the world and has undertaken several adventurous trips into relatively less traveled areas around the globe. His interests and strengths in areas outside the high-tech industry stems directly from the knowledge gained in these extensive travels. He also enjoys having quality discussions with his children, who have varied interests that directly feed into his passion, and regular association with like-minded friends and family members.

Ram and his family live in Olathe, Kansas.

ABOUT THE EDITOR

Smitha Gundavajhala is a sophomore at Monta Vista High School in Cupertino, California. Smitha loves geography and was a State finalist in the 2009 National Geographic Bee. In the same year, she placed second in the San Francisco Chronicle Scripps Spelling Bee. She placed first in spelling, and second in vocabulary and geography in other national competitions. She also received Outstanding Achievement awards for both Geography and Journalism while at Kennedy Middle School, where she was a contributing editor-in-chief of her school newspaper, the Pawpurri. She is currently on the staff of MVHS's newspaper, El Estoque, and is a captain of the Speech Team. Smitha enjoys volunteering in her free time, holding health fairs with Breathe California, and assisting with events in school and around the community with NHS, CSF, Octagon, Study Buddies, and the HealthTrust Food Basket. She has participated in several swim competitions with DACA, and has performed classical Indian music and dance around the Bay Area on multiple occasions. Smitha's interests include travel, communications, science, and design.